Thoughts on the Ne[image_ref id="1"] Improving the Condition of the Slaves in the British Colonies

With a View to Their Ultimate Emancipation And on the Practicability, the Safety, and the Advantages of the Latter Measure.

Thomas Clarkson

Alpha Editions

This edition published in 2023

ISBN : 9789357949118

Design and Setting By
Alpha Editions
www.alphaedis.com
Email - info@alphaedis.com

Contents

PREFACE.

The following sheets first appeared in a periodical work called The Inquirer. They are now republished without undergoing any substantial alteration. The author however thinks it due to himself to state, that *he would have materially qualified those parts of his essay which speak of the improved Condition of the Slaves in the West Indies since the abolition*, had he then been acquainted with the recent evidence obtained upon that subject. His present conviction certainly is, that he has overrated that improvement, and that in point of fact Negro Slavery is, in its main and leading feature, the same system which it was when the Abolition controversy first commenced.

It is possible there may be some, who, having glanced over the Title Page of this little work, may be startled at the word *Emancipation*. I wish to inform such, that Mr. Dundas, afterwards Lord Melville, an acute Man, and a Friend to the Planters, *proposed this very measure to Parliament* in the year 1792. We see, then, that the word Emancipation cannot be charged with *Novelty*. It contains now *no new ideas*. It contains now nothing but what has been *thought practicable*, and *even desirable to be accomplished*. The Emancipation which I desire is such an Emancipation only, as I firmly believe to be compatible not only with the due subordination and happiness of the labourer, but with the permanent interests of his employer.

I wish also to say, in case any thing like an undue warmth of feeling on my part should be discovered in the course of the work, that I had no intention of being warm against the West Indians as a body. I know that there are many estimable men among them living in England, who deserve every desirable praise for having sent over instructions to their Agents in the West Indies from time to time in behalf of their wretched Slaves. And yet, alas! even these, *the Masters themselves, have not had influence enough to secure the fulfilment of their own instructions upon their own estates*; nor will they, *so long as the present system continues*. They will never be able to carry their meritorious designs into effect against *Prejudice, Law, and Custom*. If this be not so, how happens it that you cannot see the Slaves, belonging to such estimable men, *without marks of the whip upon their backs?* The truth is, that *so long as overseers, drivers, and others, are entrusted with the use of arbitrary power*, and *so long as Negro-evidence is invalid against the white oppressor*, and *so long as human nature continues to be what it is*, no order from the Master for the better personal treatment of the Slave *will or can be obeyed*. It is against the *system* then, and not against the West Indians as a body, that I am warm, should I be found so unintentionally, in the present work.

One word or two now on another part of the subject. A great noise will be made, no doubt, when the question of Emancipation comes to be agitated, about *the immense property at stake*, I mean the property of the Planters;—and others connected with them. This is all well. Their interests ought undoubtedly to be attended to. But I hope and trust, that, if property is to be attended to *on one side* of the question, it will be equally attended to *on the other.* This is but common justice. If you put into one scale *the gold* and *jewels* of the Planters, you are bound to put into the other *the liberty* of 800,000 of the African race; for every man's liberty is *his own property* by the laws of *Nature, Reason, Justice,* and *Religion?* and, if it be not so with our West Indian Slaves, it *is only because* they have been, and continue to be, *deprived* of it *by force.* And here let us consider for a moment which of these two different sorts of property is of the greatest value. Let us suppose an English gentleman to be seized by ruffians on the banks of the Thames (and why not a *gentleman* when African *princes* have been so served?) and hurried away to a land (and Algiers is such a land, for instance), where white persons are held as Slaves. Now this gentleman has not been used to severe labour (neither has the African in his own country); and being therefore unable, though he does his best, to please his master, he is roused to further exertion *by the whip.* Perhaps he takes this treatment indignantly. This only secures him *a severer punishment.* I say nothing of his being badly fed, or lodged, or clothed. If he should have a wife and daughters with him, how much more cruel would be his fate! to see the tender skins of these lacerated by the whip! to see them torn from him, with a knowledge, that they are going to be compelled to submit to the lust of an overseer! *and no redress.* "How long," says he, "is this frightful system, which tears my body in pieces and excruciates my soul, which kills me by inches, and which involves my family in unspeakable misery and unmerited disgrace, to continue?"—"For *ever,*" replies a voice Suddenly: "*for ever,* as relates to your *own* life, and the life *of your wife and daughters,* and that of *all their posterity,*" Now would not this gentleman give *all that he had left behind him* in England, and *all that he had in the world besides,* and *all that he had in prospect and expectancy,* to get out of this wretched state, though he foresaw that on his return to his own country he would be obliged to beg his bread for the remainder of his life? I am sure he would. I am sure he would *instantly* prefer his *liberty to his gold.* There would not be *the hesitation of a moment* as to the choice he would make. I hope, then, that if *the argument of property* should he urged on *one side* of the question, the *argument of property (liberty) will not be overlooked on the other,* but that they will be fairly weighed, the one against the other, and that an allowance will be made as the scale shall preponderate on either side.

THOUGHTS, &c.

I know of no subject, where humanity and justice, as well as public and private interest, would be more intimately united than in that, which should recommend a mitigation of the slavery, with a view afterwards to the emancipation of the Negroes, wherever such may be held in bondage. This subject was taken up for consideration, so early as when the Abolition of the slave trade was first practically thought of, and by the very persons who first publicly embarked in that cause in England; but it was at length abandoned by them, not on the ground *that Slavery was less cruel, or wicked, or impolitic, than the slave trade*, but for other reasons. In the first place there were not at that time so many obstacles in the way of the Abolition, as of the Emancipation of the Negroes. In the second place Abolition could be effected immediately, and with but comparatively little loss, and no danger. Emancipation, on the other hand, appeared to be rather a work of time. It was beset too with many difficulties, which required deep consideration, and which, if not treated with great caution and prudence, threatened the most alarming results. In the third place, it was supposed, that, by effecting the abolition of the slave trade, the axe would be laid to the root of the whole evil; so that by cutting off the more vital part of it, the other would gradually die away:—for what was more reasonable than to suppose, that, when masters could no longer obtain Slaves from Africa or elsewhere, they would be compelled individually, by a sort of inevitable necessity, or a fear of consequences, or by a sense of their own interest, *to take better care of those whom they might then have in their possession*? What was more reasonable to suppose, than that the different legislatures themselves, moved also by the same necessity, *would immediately interfere*, without even the loss of a day, *and so alter and amend the laws* relative to the treatment of Slaves, as to enforce that as a public duty, which it would be thus the private interest of individuals to perform? Was it not also reasonable to suppose that a system of better treatment, thus begun by individuals, and enforced directly afterwards by law, would produce more willing as well as more able and valuable labourers than before; and that this effect, when once visible, would again lead both masters and legislators on the score of interest to treat their slaves still more like men; nay, at length to give them even privileges; and thus to elevate their condition by degrees, till at length it would be no difficult task, and no mighty transition, *to pass them* to that most advantageous situation to both parties, *the rank of Free Men?*

These were the three effects, which the simple measure of the abolition of the slave trade was expected to produce by those, who first espoused it, by Mr. Granville Sharp, and those who formed the London committee; and by Mr. Pitt, Mr. Fox, Mr. Burke, Mr. Wilberforce, and others of illustrious name, who brought the subject before Parliament. The question then is, how have these fond expectations been realized? or how many and which of these desirable effects have been produced? I may answer perhaps with truth, that in our own Islands, where the law of the abolition is not so easily evaded, or where there is less chance of obtaining new slaves, than in some other parts, there has been already, that is, since the abolition of the slave trade, a somewhat *better individual* treatment of the slaves than before. A certain care has been taken of them. The plough has been introduced to ease their labour. Indulgences have been given to pregnant women both before and after their delivery; premiums have been offered for the rearing of infants to a certain age; religious instruction has been allowed to many. But when I mention these instances of improvement, I must be careful to distinguish what I mean;—I do not intend to say, that there were no instances of humane treatment of the slaves before the abolition of the slave trade. I know, on the other hand, that there were; I know that there were planters, who introduced the plough upon their estates, and who much to their Honour granted similar indulgences, premiums, and permissions to those now mentioned, previously to this great event. All then that I mean to say is this, that, independently of the common progress of humanity and liberal opinion, the circumstance of not being able to get new slaves as formerly, has had its influence upon some of our planters; that it has made some of them think more; that it has put some of them more upon their guard; and that there are therefore upon the whole, more instances of good treatment of slaves by individuals in our Islands (though far from being as numerous as they ought to be) than at any former period.

But, alas! though the abolition of the slave trade may have produced a somewhat better individual treatment of the slaves, and this also to a somewhat greater extent than formerly, *not one of the other effects*, so anxiously looked for, has been realized. The condition of the slaves has not yet been improved by *law*. It is a remarkable, and indeed almost an incredible fact, *that no one effort has been made* by the legislative bodies in our Islands with *the real* intention of meeting the new, the great, and the extraordinary event of the abolition of the slave trade. While indeed this measure was under discussion by the British Parliament, an attempt was made in several of our Islands to alter the old laws with a view, as it was then pretended, of providing better for the wants and personal protection of the slaves; but it was afterwards discovered, that the promoters of this alteration never meant to carry it into effect. It was intended, by making a show of these laws, *to deceive the people of England*, and *thus to prevent them from following up the great question of the abolition*. Mr. Clappeson, one of the evidences examined by the House of Commons, was in Jamaica, when the Assembly passed their famous consolidated laws, and he told the House, that "he had often heard from people there, that it was passed because of the stir in England about the slave trade;" and he added, "that slaves continued to be as ill treated there *since the passing of that act as before.*" Mr. Cook, another of the evidences examined, was long resident in the same island, and, "though he lived there also *since the passing of the* act, *he knew of no legal protection,* which slaves had against injuries from their masters." Mr. Dalrymple was examined to the same point for Grenada. He was there in 1788, when the Act for that island was passed also, called "An Act for the better Protection and promoting the Increase and Population of Slaves." He told the House, that, "while he resided there, the proposal in the British Parliament for the abolition of the slave trade was a matter of general discussion, and that he believed, that this was a principal reason for passing it. He was of opinion, however, that this Act would prove ineffectual, because, as Negro evidence was not to be admitted, those, who chose to abuse their slaves, might still do it with impunity; and people, who lived on terms of intimacy, would dislike the idea of becoming spies and informers against each other." We have the same account of the ameliorating Act of Dominica. "This Act," says Governor Prevost, "appears to have been considered from the day it was passed until this hour as *a political measure to avert the interference of the mother country in the management of the slaves.*" We, are informed also on the same authority, that the clauses of this Act, which had given a promise of better days, "*had been wholly neglected.*" In short, the Acts passed in our different Islands for the pretended purpose of bettering the condition of the slaves have been all of them most shamefully neglected; and they remain only a dead letter; or they are as much a nullity, as if they had never existed, at the present day.

And as our planters have done nothing yet effectively by *law* for ameliorating the condition of their slaves, so they have done nothing or worse than nothing in the case of their *emancipation.* In the year 1815 Mr. Wilberforce gave notice in the House of Commons of his intention to introduce there a bill for the registration of slaves in the British colonies. In the following year an insurrection broke out among some slaves in Barbadoes. Now, though this insurrection originated, as there was then reason to believe, in local or peculiar circumstances, or in circumstances which had often produced insurrections before, the planters chose to attribute it to the Registry Bill now mentioned. They gave out also, that the slaves in Jamaica and in the other islands had imbibed a notion, that this Bill was to lead to *their emancipation*; that, while this notion existed, their minds would be in an unsettled state; and therefore that it was necessary that *it should be done away.* Accordingly on the 19th day of June 1816, they moved and procured an address from the Commons to the Prince Regent, the substance of which was (as relates to this particular) that "His Royal Highness would be pleased to order all the governors of the West India islands to proclaim, in the most public manner, His Royal Highness's concern and surprise at the false and mischievous opinion, which appeared to have prevailed in some of the British colonies,—

that either His Royal Highness or the British Parliament had sent out orders for *the emancipation* of the Negroes; and to direct the most effectual methods to be adopted for discountenancing *these unfounded and dangerous impressions.*" Here then we have a proof "that in the month of June 1816 the planters *had no notion of altering the condition of their Negroes.*" It is also evident, that they have entertained *no such notion since*, for emancipation implies a *preparation* of the persons who are to be the subjects of so great a change. It implies a previous alteration of treatment for the better, and a previous alteration of customs and even of circumstances, no one of which can however be really and truly effected without *a previous change of the laws.* In fact, a progressively better treatment *by law* must have been settled as a preparatory and absolutely necessary work, had *emancipation been intended.* But as we have never heard of the introduction of any new laws to this effect, or with a view of producing this effect, in any of our colonies, we have an evidence, almost as clear as the sun at noonday, that our planters have no notion of altering the condition of their Negroes, though fifteen years have elapsed since the abolition of the slave trade. But if it be true that the abolition of the slave trade has not produced all the effects, which the abolitionists anticipated or intended, it would appear to be their duty, unless insurmountable obstacles present themselves, *to resume their labours:* for though there may be upon the whole, as I have admitted, a somewhat better *individual* treatment of the slaves by their masters, arising out of an increased prudence in same, which has been occasioned by stopping the importations, yet it is true, that not only many of the former continue to be ill-treated by the latter, but that *all may be so ill-treated*, if the *latter be so disposed.* They may be ill-fed, hard-worked, ill-used, and wantonly and barbarously punished. They may be tortured, nay even deliberately and intentionally killed without the means of redress, or the punishment of the aggressor, so long as the evidence of a Negro is not valid against a white man. If a white master only take care, that no other white man sees him commit an atrocity of the kind mentioned, he is safe from the cognizance of the law. He may commit such atrocity in the sight of a thousand black spectators, and no harm will happen to him from it. In fact, the slaves in our Islands have *no more real protection or redress from law*, than when *the Abolitionists first took up the question of the slave trade.* It is evident therefore, that the latter have still one-half of their work to perform, and that it is their duty to perform it. If they were ever influenced by any good motives, whether of humanity, justice, or religion, to undertake the cause of the Negroes, they must even now be influenced by the same motives to continue it. If any of those disorders still exist, which it was their intention to cure, they cannot (if these are curable) retire from the course and say—there is now no further need of our interference.

The first step then to be taken by the Abolitionists is to attempt to introduce an *entire new code of laws* into our colonies. The treatment of the Negroes there must no longer be made to depend upon *the presumed effects* of the abolition of the slave trade. Indeed there were persons well acquainted with Colonial concerns, who called the abolition *but a half measure* at the time when it was first publicly talked of. They were sure, that it would never *of itself* answer the end proposed. Mr. Steele also confessed in his letter to Dr. Dickson[1] (of both of whom more by and by), that "the abolition of the stave trade would *be useless*, unless at the same time the infamous laws, which he had pointed out, *were repealed*." Neither must the treatment of the Negroes be made to depend upon what may be called *contingent humanity*. We now leave in this country neither the horse, nor the ass, nor oxen, nor sheep, to the contingent humanity even of *British bosoms*;—and shall we leave those, whom we have proved to be *men*, to the contingent humanity of a *slave colony*, where the eye is familiarized with cruel sights, and where we have seen a constant exposure to oppression without the possibility of redress? No. The treatment of the Negroes must be made to depend *upon law*; and unless this be done, we shall look in vain for any real amelioration of their condition. In the first place, all those old laws, which are repugnant to humanity and justice, must be done away. There must also be new laws, positive, certain, easy of execution, binding upon all, by means of which the Negroes in our islands shall have speedy and substantial redress in real cases of ill-usage, whether by starvation, over-work, or acts of personal violence, or otherwise. There must be new laws again more akin to the principle of *reward* than of *punishment*, of *privilege* than of *privation*, and which shall, have a tendency to raise or elevate their condition, so as to fit them by degrees to sustain the rank of free men.

But if a new Code of Laws be indispensably necessary in our colonies in order to secure a better treatment to the slaves, to whom must we look for it? I answer, that we must not look for it to the West Indian Legislatures. For, in the first place, judging of what they are likely to do from what they have already done, or rather from what they have *not* done, we can have no reasonable expectation from that quarter. One hundred and fifty years have passed, during which long interval their laws have been nearly stationary, or without any material improvement. In the second place, the individuals composing these Legislatures, having been used to the exercise of unlimited power, would be unwilling to part with that portion of it, which would be necessary to secure the object in view. In the third place, their prejudices against their slaves are too great to allow them to become either impartial or willing actors in the case. The term *slave* being synonymous according to their estimation and usage with the term *brute*, they have fixed a stigma upon their Negroes, such as we, who live in Europe, could not have conceived, unless we had had irrefragable evidence upon the point. What evils has not this cruel association of terms produced? The West Indian master looks down upon his slave with disdain. He has besides a certain antipathy against him. He hates the sight of his features, and of his colour; nay, he marks with distinctive opprobrium the very blood in his veins, attaching different names and more or less infamy to those who have it in them, according to the quantity which they have of it in consequence of their pedigree, or of their greater or less degree of consanguinity with the whites. Hence the West Indian feels an unwillingness to elevate the condition of the Negro, or to do any thing for him as a human being. I have no doubt, that this prejudice has been one of the great causes why the improvement of our slave population *by law* has been so long retarded, and that the same prejudice will continue to have a similar operation, so long as it shall continue to exist. Not that there are wanting men of humanity among our West Indian legislators. Their humanity is discernible enough when it is to be applied to the *whites*; but such is the system of slavery, and the degradation attached to this system, that their humanity seems to be lost or gone, when it is to be applied to the *blacks*. Not again that there are wanting men of sense among the same body. They are shrewd and clever enough in the affairs of life, where they maintain an intercourse with the *whites*; but in their intercourse with the *blacks* their sense appears to be shrivelled and not of its ordinary size. Look at the laws of their own making, as far as the Negroes are concerned, and they are a collection of any thing but—wisdom.

It appears then, that if a new code of laws is indispensably necessary in our Colonies in order to secure a better treatment of the slaves there, we are not to look to the West Indian Legislatures for it. To whom then are we to turn our eyes for help on this occasion? We answer, To the British Parliament, the source of all legitimate power; to that Parliament, *which has already heard and redressed in part the wrongs of Africa*. The West Indian Legislatures must be called upon to send their respective codes to this Parliament for revision. Here they will be well and impartially examined; some of the laws will be struck out, others amended, and others added; and at length they will be returned to the Colonies, means having been previously devised for their execution there.

But here no doubt a considerable opposition would arise on the part of the West India planters. These would consider any such interference by the British Parliament as an invasion of their rights, and they would cry out accordingly. We remember that they set up a clamour when the abolition of the slave trade was first proposed. But what did Mr. Pitt say to them in the House of Commons? "I will now," said he, "consider the proposition, that on account of some patrimonial rights of the West Indians, the prohibition of the slave trade would be an invasion of their legal inheritance. This proposition implied, that Parliament had no right to stop the importations: but had this detestable traffic received such a sanction, as placed it more out of the jurisdiction of the Legislature for ever after, than any other branch of our trade? But if the laws respecting the slave trade implied a contract for its perpetual continuance, the House could never regulate any other of the branches of our national commerce. But *any contract* for the promotion of this trade must, in his opinion, *have been void from the beginning;* for if it was *an outrage upon justice,* and only another name for *fraud, robbery, and murder,* what *pledge* could devolve upon the Legislature to incur the obligation of becoming principals in the commission of such enormities by sanctioning their continuance?"

They set up again a similar clamour, when the Registry Bill before mentioned was discussed in Parliament, contending that the introduction of it there was an interference with their rights also: but we must not forget the reply which Mr. Canning made to them on that occasion. "He had known, (he said,) and there might again occur, instances of obstinacy in the colonial assemblies, which left the British Parliament no choice but direct interference. Such conduct might now call for such an exertion on the part of Parliament; but all that he pleaded for was, that time should be granted, that it might be known if the colonial assemblies would take upon them to do what that House was pleased to declare should be done. The present address could not be misunderstood. It told the colonial assemblies, You are safe for the present from the interference of the British Parliament, on the belief, and on the promise made for you, that left to yourselves you will do what is required of you. To hold this language was sufficient. The Assemblies might be left to infer the consequences of a refusal, and Parliament might rest satisfied with the consciousness, that they held in their hands the means of accomplishing that which they had proposed." In a subsequent discussion of the subject in the House of Lords, Lord Holland remarked, that "in his opinion there had been more prejudice against this Bill than the nature of the thing justified; but, whatever might be the objection felt against it in the Colonies, it might be well for them to consider, that it would be *impossible for them to resist,* and that, if the thing was not done by them, *it would be done for them.*" But on this subject, that is, on the subject of colonial rights, I shall say more in another place. It will be proper, however, to repeat here, and to insist upon it too, that there is no *effectual way* of remedying the evil complained of, but by subjecting the colonial laws to the *revision of the Legislature of the mother country;* and perhaps I shall disarm some of the opponents to this measure, and at any rate free myself from the charge of a novel and wild proposition, when I inform them that Mr. Long, the celebrated historian and planter of Jamaica, and to whose authority all West Indians look up, adopted the same idea. Writing on the affairs of Jamaica, he says: "The system[2] of Colonial government, and the imperfection of their several laws, are subjects, which never were, but *which ought to be,* strictly canvassed, examined, and amended by the British Parliament."

The second and last step to be taken by the Abolitionists should be, to collect all possible light on the subject of *emancipation* with a view of carrying that measure into effect in its due time. They ought never to forget, that *emancipation* was included in *their original idea of the abolition of the slave trade.* Slavery was then as much an evil in their eyes as the trade itself; and so long as the former continues in its present state, the extinction of it ought to be equally an object of their care. All the slaves in our colonies, whether men, women, or children, whether *Africans or Creoles,* have been unjustly deprived of their rights. There is not a master, who has the least claim to their services in point of equity. There is, therefore, a great debt due to them, and for this no payment, no amends, no equivalent can be found, but a *restoration to their liberty.*

That all have been unjustly deprived of their rights, may be easily shown by examining the different grounds on which they are alleged to be held in bondage. With respect to those in our colonies, who are *Africans,* I never heard of any title to them but by the *right of purchase.* But it will be asked, where did the purchasers get them? It will be answered, that they got them from the sellers; and where did the sellers, that is, the original sellers, get them? They got them by *fraud or violence.* So says the evidence before the House of Commons; and so, in fact, said both Houses of Parliament, when they abolished the trade: and this is the plea set up for retaining them in a cruel bondage!!!

With respect to the rest of the slaves, that is, the *Creoles,* or those born in the colonies, the services, the perpetual services, of these are claimed on the plea of the *law of birth.* They were born slaves, and this circumstance is said to give to their masters a sufficient right to their persons. But this doctrine sprung from the old Roman law, which taught that all slaves were to be considered as *cattle.* "Partus sequitur ventrem," says this law, or the "condition or lot of the mother determines the condition or lot of the offspring." It is the same law, which we ourselves now apply to cattle while they are in our possession. Thus the calf belongs to the man who owns the cow, and the foal to the man who owns the mare, and not to the owner of the bull or horse, which were the male parents of each. It is then upon this, the old Roman law, and not upon any English law, that the planters found their right to the services of such as are born in slavery. In conformity with this law they denied, for one hundred and fifty years, both the moral and intellectual nature of their slaves. They considered them themselves, and they wished them to be considered by others, in these respects, as upon a level only *with the beasts of the field.* Happily, however, their efforts have been in vain. The evidence examined before the House of Commons in the years 1789, 1790, and 1791, has confirmed the falsehood of their doctrines. It has proved that the social affections and the intellectual powers both of Africans and Creoles are the same as those of other human beings. What then becomes of the Roman law? For as it takes no other view of slaves than as *cattle*, how is it applicable to those, whom we have so abundantly proved *to be men*?

This is the grand plea, upon which our West Indian planters have founded their right to the perpetual services of their *Creole* slaves. They consider them as the young or offspring of cattle. But as the slaves in question have been proved, and are now acknowledged, to be the offspring of men and women, of social, intellectual, and accountable beings, their right must fall to the ground. Nor do I know upon what other principle or right they can support it. They can have surely no *natural right* to the infant, who is born of a woman slave. If there be any right to it by *nature*, such right must belong, not to the master of the mother, but to the mother herself. They can have no right to it again, either on the score of *reason* or of *justice*. Debt and crime have been generally admitted to be two fair grounds, on which men may be justly deprived of their liberty for a time, and even made to labour, inasmuch as they include *reparation of injury*, and the duty of the magistrate to *make examples*, in order that he may not bear the sword in vain. But what injury had the infant done, when it came into the world, to the master of its mother, that reparation should be sought for, or punishment inflicted for example, and that this reparation and this punishment should be made to consist of a course of action and suffering, against which, more than against any other, human nature would revolt? Is it reasonable, is it just, that a poor infant who has done no injury to any one, should be subjected, *he and his posterity for ever*, to *the arbitrary will and tyranny of another*, and moreover to *the condition of a brute*, because by *mere accident*, and by *no fault* or *will of his own*, he was born of a person, who had been previously in the condition of a slave?

And as the right to slaves, because they were born slaves, cannot be defended either upon the principles of reason or of justice, so this right absolutely falls to pieces, when we come to try it by the touchstone *of the Christian religion*. Every man who is born into the world, whether he be white or whether he be black, is born, according to Christian notions, a *free agent* and *an accountable creature*. This is the Scriptural law of his nature as a human bring. He is born under this law, and he continues under it during his life. Now the West Indian slavery is of such an arbitrary nature, that it may be termed *proper* or *absolute*. The dominion attached to it is a despotism without control; a despotism, which keeps up its authority by terror only. The subjects of it *must do*, and this *instantaneously*, whatever their master *orders them to do*, whether it *be right or wrong*. His will, and his will alone, is their law. If the wife of a slave were ordered by a master to submit herself to his lusts, and therefore to commit adultery, or if her husband were ordered to steal any thing for him, and therefore to commit theft, I have no conception that either the one or the other would *dare* to disobey his commands. "The whip, the shackles, the dungeon," says Mr. Steele before mentioned, "are at all times in his power, whether it be to gratify his *lust*, or display his authority[3]." Now if the master has the power, *a just, and moral power*, to make his slaves do what he orders them to do, even if it be wrong, then I must contend that the Scriptures, whose authority we venerate, are false. I must contend that his slaves never could have been born free agents and accountable creatures; or that, as soon as they became slaves, they were absolved from the condition of free-agency and that they lost their responsibility as men. But if, on the other hand, it be the revealed will of God, that all men, without exception, must be left free to act, but accountable to God for their actions;—I contend that no man can be born, nay, further, that no man can be made, held, or possessed, as a proper slave. I contend that there can be, according to the Gospel-dispensation, *no such state as West Indian slavery*. But let us now suppose for a moment, that there might be found an instance or two of slaves enlightened by some pious Missionary, who would refuse to execute their master's orders on the principle that they were wrong; even this would not alter our views of the case. For would not this refusal be so unexampled, so unlooked-for, so immediately destructive to all authority and discipline, and so provocative of anger, that it would be followed by *immediate and signal punishment?* Here then we should have a West Indian master reversing all the laws and rules of civilized nations, and turning upside down all the morality of the Gospel by the novel practice of *punishing men for their virtues*. This new case affords another argument, why a man cannot be born a proper slave. In fact, the whole system of our planters appears to me to be so directly in opposition to the whole system of our religion, that I have no conception, how a man can have been born a slave, such as the West Indian is; nor indeed have I any conception, how he can be, rightly, or justly, or properly, a West Indian slave at all. There appears to me something even impious in the thought; and I am convinced, that many years will not pass, before the West Indian slavery will fall, and that future ages will contemplate with astonishment how the preceding could have tolerated it.

It has now appeared, if I have reasoned conclusively, that the West Indians have no title to their slaves on the ground of purchase, nor on the plea of the law of birth, nor on that of any natural right, nor on that of reason or justice, and that Christianity absolutely annihilates it. It remains only to show, that they have no title to them on the ground of *original grants or permissions of Governments*, or of *Acts of Parliament*, or of *Charters*, or of *English law*.

With respect to original grants or permissions of Governments, the case is very clear. History informs us, that neither the African slave trade nor the West Indian slavery would have been allowed, had it not been for the *misrepresentations* and *falsehoods* of those, *who were first concerned in them*. The Governments of those times were made to believe, first, that the poor

Africans embarked *voluntarily* on board the ships which took them from their native land; and secondly, that they were conveyed to the Colonies principally for *their own benefit*, or out of *Christian feeling for them*, that they might afterwards *be converted to Christianity*. Take as an instance of the first assertion, the way in which Queen Elizabeth was deceived, in whose reign the execrable slave trade began in England. This great princess seems on the very commencement of the trade to have questioned its lawfulness. She seems to have entertained a religious scruple concerning it, and indeed, to have revolted at the very thoughts of it. She seems to have been aware of the evils to which its continuance might lead, or that, if it were sanctioned, the most unjustifiable means might be made use of to procure the persons of the natives of Africa. And in what light she would have viewed any acts of this kind, had they taken place to her knowledge, we may conjecture from this fact—that when Captain (afterwards Sir John) Hawkins returned from his first voyage to Africa and Hispaniola, whither he had carried slaves, she sent for him, and, as we learn from Hill's Naval History, expressed her concern lest any of the Africans should be carried off *without their free consent*, declaring, "that it would be detestable and call down the vengeance of Heaven upon the undertakers." Capt. Hawkins promised to comply with the injunctions of Elizabeth in this respect. But he did not keep his word; for when he went to Africa again, *he seized* many of the inhabitants *and carried them off* as slaves, "Here (says Hill) began the horrid practice of forcing the Africans into slavery, an injustice and barbarity, which, so sure as there is vengeance in Heaven for the worst of crimes, will sometime be the destruction of all who encourage it." Take as an instance of the second what Labat, a Roman missionary, records in his account of the Isles of America. He says, that Louis the Thirteenth was very uneasy, when he was about to issue the edict, by which all Africans coming into his colonies were to be made slaves; and that this uneasiness continued, till he was assured that the introduction of them in this capacity into his foreign dominions was the readiest way of *converting them* to the principles *of the Christian religion*. It was upon these ideas then, namely, that the Africans left their own country voluntarily, and that they were to receive the blessings of Christianity, and upon these alone, that the first transportations were allowed, and that the first *English* grants and Acts of Parliament, and that the first *foreign* edicts, sanctioned them. We have therefore the fact well authenticated, as it relates *to original Government grants and permissions*, that the owners of many of the Creole slaves in our colonies have no better title to them as property, than as being the descendants of persons forced away from their country and brought thither by a traffic, which had its allowed origin in *fraud and falsehood*.

Neither have the masters of slaves in our colonies any title to their slaves on account of any *charters*, which they may be able to produce, though their charters are the only source of their power. It is through these that they have hitherto legislated, and that they continue to legislate. Take away their charters, and they would have no right or power to legislate at all. And yet, though they have their charters, and though the slavery, which now exists, has been formed and kept together entirely by the laws, which such charters have given them the power to make, this very slavery *is illegal.* There is not an individual, who holds any of the slaves by a *legal* title: for it is expressed in all these charters, whether in those given to William Penn and others for the continent of North America, or in those given for the islands now under our consideration, that "the laws and statutes, to be made there, are *not to be repugnant,* but, as near as may be, *agreeable, to the laws* and statutes of this our *kingdom of Great Britain.*" But is it consistent with the laws of England, that any one man should have the power of forcing another to work for him without wages? Is it consistent with the laws of England, that any one man should have the power of flogging, beating, bruising, or wounding another at his discretion? Is it consistent with the laws of England, that a man should be judged by any but his peers? Is it consistent with the same laws, that a man should be deprived of the power of giving evidence against the man who has injured him? or that there should be a privileged class, against whom no testimony can be admitted on certain occasions, though the perpetrators of the most horrid crimes? But when we talk of consistency on this occasion, let us not forget that old law of Barbadoes, made while the charter of that island was fresh in every body's memory, and therefore in the very teeth of the charter itself, which runs thus: "If any slave, under punishment by his master or by his order, shall suffer in life or member, no person shall be liable to any fine for the same: but if any person shall *wantonly* or *cruelly* kill his own slave, he shall pay the treasury 15*l.*" And here let us remark, that, when Lord Seaforth, governor of Barbadoes, proposed, so lately as in 1802, the repeal of this bloody law, the Legislature of that island rejected the proposition with indignation. Nay, the very proposal to repeal it so stirred up at the time the bad passions of many, that several brutal murders of slaves were committed in consequence; and it was not till two or three years afterwards that the governor had influence enough to get the law repealed. Let the West Indians then talk no more of their *charters;* for in consequence of having legislated upon principles, which are at variance with those upon which the laws of England are founded, they have *forfeited them all.* The mother country has therefore a right to withdraw these charters whenever she pleases, and to substitute such others as she may think proper. And here let it be observed also, that the right of the West Indians to make any laws at all for their own islands being founded upon their charters, and upon these alone, and the laws relating to the slaves being contrary to what such charters prescribe, the *slavery itself,* that is, the daily living practice with respect to slaves under such laws, *is illegal* and *may be done away.* But if so, all our West Indian slaves are, without exception, unlawfully held in bondage. There is no master, who has a legal title to any of them. This assertion may appear strange and extravagant to many; but it does not follow on that account that it is the less true. It is an assertion, which has been made by a West Indian proprietor himself. Mr. Steele[4], before quoted, furnishes us with what passed at the meeting of the Society of Arts in Barbadoes at their committee-room in August 1785, when the following question was in the order of the day: "Is there any law written, or printed, by which a proprietor can prove his title to his slave under or conformable to the laws of England?" And "Why, (immediately said one of the members,) why conformable to the laws of England? Will not the courts in England admit such proof as is authorized by *our slave laws*?"—"I apprehend not, (answered a second,) unless we can show that *our slave laws* (according to the limitations of the charter) are *not* repugnant to the laws of England."—The same gentleman resumed: "Does the original purchaser of an African slave in this island obtain any legal title from the merchant or importer of slaves—and of what nature? Does it set forth any title of propriety, agreeable to the laws of England (or even to the laws of nations) to be in the importer more than what depends upon his simple averment? And have not free Negroes been at sundry times trepanned by such dealers, and been brought contrary to the laws of nations, and sold here as slaves?"— "There is no doubt, (observed a third,) but such villainous actions have been done by worthless people: however, though an honest and unsuspicious man may be deceived in buying a stolen horse, it does not follow that he may not have a fair and just title to a horse or any thing else bought in an open and legal market; but according to the obligation *of being not repugnant to the laws of England,* I do not see how *we can have any title to our slaves* likely to be supported by the laws of England." In fact, the Colonial system is an excrescence upon the English Constitution, and is constantly at variance with it. There is not one English law, which gives a man a right to the liberty of any of his fellow creatures. Of course there cannot be, according to charters, any Colonial law to this effect. If there be, it is *null and void.* Nay, the very man, who is held in bondage by the Colonial law, becomes free by English law the moment he reaches the English shore. But we have said enough for our present purpose. We have shown that the slaves in our Colonies, whether they be Africans, or whether they be Creoles, *have been unjustly deprived of their rights.* There is of course a great debt due to them. They have a claim to a restoration to liberty; and as this restoration was included by the Abolitionists in their original idea of the abolition of the slavetrade, so it is their duty to endeavour to obtain it *the first moment it is practicable.* I shall conclude my observations on this part of the subject, in the words of that old champion of African liberty, Mr. W. Smith, the present Member for Norwich, when addressing the House of Commons in the last session of parliament on a particular occasion. He admitted, alluding to the slaves in our colonies, that "immediate emancipation might be an injury, and not a blessing to the slaves themselves.

A period of *preparation*, which unhappily included delay, seemed to be necessary. The ground of this delay, however, was not the intermediate advantage to be derived from their labour, but a conviction of its expediency as it related to themselves. We had to *compensate* to these wretched beings *for ages of injustice*. We were bound by the strongest obligations *to train up* these subjects of our past injustice and tyranny *for an equal participation with ourselves in the blessings of liberty and the protection of the law*; and by these considerations ought our measures to be strictly and conscientiously regulated. It was only in consequence of the necessity of time to be consumed in such a preparation, that we could be justified in the retention of the Negroes in slavery *for a single hour*; and he trusted that the eyes of all men, both here and in the colonies, would be open to this view of the subject as their clear and indispensable duty."

Having led the reader to the first necessary step to be taken in favour of our slaves in the British Colonies,—namely, the procuring for them a new and better code of laws; and having since led him to the last or final one,—namely, the procuring for them the rights of which they have been unjustly deprived: I shall now confine myself entirely to this latter branch of the subject, being assured, that it has a claim to all the attention that can be bestowed upon it; and I trust that I shall be able to show, by appealing to historical facts, that however awful and tremendous the work of *emancipation* may seem, it is yet *practicable*; that it is practicable also *without danger*, and moreover, that it is practicable with the probability of *advantage* to all the parties concerned.

In appealing however to facts for this purpose, we must expect no light from antiquity to guide us on our way; for history gives us no account of persons in those times similarly situated with the slaves in the British colonies at the present day. There were no particular nations in those times, like the Africans, expressly set apart for slavery by the rest of the world, so as to have a stigma put upon them on that account, nor did a difference of the colour of the skin constitute always, as it now does, a most marked distinction between the master and the slave, so as to increase this stigma and to perpetuate antipathies between them. Nor did the slaves of antiquity, except perhaps once in Sparta, form the whole labouring population of the land; nor did they work incessantly, like the Africans, under the whip; nor were they generally so behind their masters in cultivated intellect. Neither does ancient history give us in the cases of manumission, which it records, any parallel, from which we might argue in the case before us. The ancient manumissions were those of individuals only, generally of but one at a time, and only now and then; whereas the emancipation, which we contemplate in the colonies, will comprehend *whole bodies of men*, nay, *whole populations*, at a given time. We must go therefore in quest of examples to modern times, or rather to the history of the colonial slavery itself; and if we should find any there, which appear to bear at all upon the case in question, we must be thankful for them, and, though they should not be entirely to our mind, we must not turn them away, but keep them, and reason from them as far as their analogies will warrant.

In examining a period comprehending the last forty years, I find no less than six or seven instances of the emancipation of African slaves *in bodies*. The first of these cases occurred at the close of the first American war. A number of slaves had run away from their North American masters and joined the British army. When peace came, the British Government did not know what to do with them. Their services were no longer wanted. To leave them behind to fall again into the power of their masters would have been great cruelty as well as injustice; and as to taking them to England, what could have been done with them there? It was at length determined to give *them their liberty*, and to disband them in Nova Scotia, and to settle them there upon grants of land as *British subjects* and as *free men*. The Nova Scotians on learning their destination were alarmed. They could not bear the thought of having such a number of black persons among them, and particularly as these understood the use of arms. The Government, however, persevering in its original intention, they were conveyed to Halifax, and distributed from thence into the country. Their number, comprehending men, women, and children, were two thousand and upwards. To gain their livelihood, some of them worked upon little portions of land of their own; others worked as carpenters; others became fishermen; and others worked for hire in other ways. In process of time they raised places of worship of their own, and had ministers of their own from their own body. They led a harmless life, and gained the character of an industrious and honest people from their white neighbours. A few years afterwards the land in Nova Scotia being found too poor to answer, and the climate too cold for their constitutions, a number of them, to the amount of between thirteen and fourteen hundred, volunteered to form a new colony, which was then first thought of, at Sierra Leone. Accordingly, having been conveyed there, they realized the object in view; and they are to be found there, they or their descendants, most of them in independent and some of them in affluent circumstances, at the present day.

A second case may be taken from what occurred at the close of the second, or last American war. It may be remembered that a large British naval force, having on board a powerful land force, sailed in the year 1814, to make a descent on the coast of the southern States of America. The British army, when landed, marched to Washington, and burnt most of its public buildings. It was engaged also at different times with the American army in the field. During these expeditions, some hundreds of slaves in these parts joined the British standard by invitation. When the campaign was over, the same difficulty occurred about disposing of these as in the former case. It was determined at length to ship them to Trinidad *as free labourers*. But here, that is, at Trinidad, an objection was started against receiving them, but on a different ground from that which had been started in the similar case in Nova Scotia. The planters of Trinidad were sure that no free Negroes would ever work, and therefore that the slaves in question would, if made free and settled among them, support themselves *by plunder*. Sir Ralph Woodford, however, the governor of the island, resisted the outcry of these prejudices. He received them into the island, and settled them where he supposed the experiment would be most safely made. The result has shown his discernment. These very men, formerly slaves in the Southern States of America and afterwards emancipated in a body at Trinidad, are now earning their own livelihood, and with so much industry and good conduct that the calumnies originally spread against them have entirely died away.

A third case may comprehend those Negroes, who lately formed what we call our West Indian black regiments. Some of these had been originally purchased in Africa, not as slaves but recruits, and others in Jamaica and elsewhere. They had all served as soldiers in the West Indies. At length certain of these regiments were transported to Sierra Leone and disbanded there, and the individuals composing them received their discharge *as free men*. This happened in the spring of 1819. *Many hundreds* of them were *set at liberty at once* upon this occasion. Some of these were afterwards marched into the interior, where they founded Waterloo, Hastings, and other villages. Others were shipped to the Isles de Loss, where they made settlements in like manner. Many, in both cases, took with them their wives, which they had brought from the West Indies, and others selected wives from the natives on the spot. They were all settled upon grants given them by the Government. It appears from accounts received from Sir Charles M'Carthy, the governor of Sierra Leone, that they have conducted themselves to his satisfaction, and that they will prove a valuable addition to that colony.

A fourth case may comprehend what we call *the captured Negroes* in the colony now mentioned. These are totally distinct from those either in the first or in the last of the cases which have been mentioned. It is well known that these were taken out of slave-ships captured at different times from the commencement of the abolition of the slave trade to the present moment, and that on being landed *they were made free*. After having been recruited in their health they were marched in bodies into the interior, where they were taught to form villages and to cultivate land for themselves. They were *made free* as they were landed from the vessels, *from fifty to two or three hundred at a time*. They occupy at present twelve towns, in which they have both their churches and their schools. Regents Town having been one of the first established, containing about thirteen hundred souls, stands foremost in improvement, and has become a pattern for industry and good example. The people there have now fallen entirely into the habits of English society. They are decently and respectably dressed. They attend divine worship regularly. They exhibit an orderly and moral conduct. In their town little shops are now beginning to make their appearance; and their lands show the marks of extraordinary cultivation. Many of them, after having supplied their own wants for the year, have a surplus produce in hand for the purchase of superfluities or comforts.

Here then are four cases of slaves, either Africans or descendants of Africans, *emancipated* in *considerable bodies* at a time. I have kept them by themselves, became they are of a different complexion from those, which I intend should follow. I shall now reason upon them. Let me premise, however, that I shall consider the three first of the cases as one, so that the same reasoning will do for all. They are alike indeed in their *main* features; and we must consider this as sufficient; for to attend minutely to every shade of difference[5], which may occur in every case, would be to bewilder the reader, and to swell the size of my work unnecessarily, or without conferring an adequate benefit to the controversy on either side.

It will be said then (for my reasoning will consist principally in answering objections on the present occasion) that the three first cases *are not strictly analogous* to that of our West Indian slaves, whose emancipation we are seeking. It will be contended, that the slaves in our West Indian colonies have been constantly in an abject and degraded state. Their faculties are benumbed. They have contracted all the vices of slavery. They are become habitually thieves and liars. Their bosoms burn with revenge against the whites. How then can persons in such a state be fit to receive their freedom? The slaves, on the other hand, who are comprehended in the three cases above mentioned, found in the British army a school as it were, *which fitted them by degrees for making a good use of their liberty*. While they were there, they were never out of the reach of discipline, and yet were daily left to themselves to act as free men. They obtained also in this *preparatory school* some knowledge of the customs of civilized life. They were in the habit also of mixing familiarly with the white soldiers. Hence, it will be said, they were in a state much *more favourable for undergoing a change in their condition* than the West Indian slaves before mentioned. I admit all this. I admit the difference between the two situations, and also the preference which I myself should give to the one above the other on account of its desirable tendencies. But I never stated, that our West Indian slaves were to be emancipated *suddenly*, but *by degrees*. I always, on the other hand, took it for granted, that they were to have *their preparatory school* also. Nor must it be forgotten, as a comparison has been instituted, that if there was *less danger* in emancipating the other slaves, *because they had received something like a preparatory education* for the change, there was *far more* in another point of view, because *they were all acquainted with the use of arms*. This is a consideration of great importance; but particularly when we consider *the prejudices of the blacks against the whites*; for would our West Indian planters be as much at their ease, as they now are, if their slaves had acquired *a knowledge of the use of arms*, or would they think them on this account more or less fit for emancipation?

It will be said again, that the fourth case, consisting of the Sierra Leone captured Negroes, *is not strictly analogous* to the one in point. These had probably been slaves but *for a short time*,—say a few months, including the time which elapsed between their reduction to slavery and their embarkation from Africa, and between this their embarkation and their capture upon the ocean. They had scarcely been slaves when they were returned to the rank of free men. Little or no change therefore could have been effected in so short an interim in their disposition and their character; and, as they were never carried to the West Indies, so they never could have contracted the bad habits, or the degradation or vices, of the slavery there. It will be contended therefore, that they were *better, or less hazardous*, subjects for *emancipation*, than the slaves in our colonies. I admit this objection, and I give it its full weight. I admit it to be *less hazardous* to emancipate a *new* than an *old* slave. And yet the case of the Sierra Leone captured Negroes is a very strong one. They were all *Africans*. They were all *slaves*. They must have contracted *as mortal a hatred of the whites* from their sufferings on board ship by fetters, whips, and suffocation in the hold, as the West Indian from those severities which are attached to their bondage upon shore. Under these circumstances then we find them *made free*; but observe, not after any *preparatory* discipline, but almost *suddenly*, and *not singly*, but *in bodies* at a time. We find them also settled or made to live under the *unnatural* government of the *whites*; and, what is more extraordinary, we find their present number, as compared with that of the whites in the same colony, nearly as *one hundred and fifty to one*; notwithstanding which superiority fresh emancipations are constantly taking place, as fresh cargoes of the captured arrive in port.

It will be said, lastly, that all the four cases put together prove nothing. They can give us nothing like *a positive assurance*, that the Negro slaves in our colonies would pass through the ordeal of emancipation without danger to their masters or the community at large. Certainly not. Nor if these instances had been far more numerous than they are, could they, in this world of accidents, have given us *a moral certainty of this*. They afford us however *a hope*, that emancipation is practicable without danger: for will any one pretend to say, that we should have had as much reason for entertaining such a hope, *if no such instances had occurred*; or that we should not have had reason to despair, *if four such experiments had been made, and if they had all failed?* They afford us again ground for believing, that there is a peculiar softness, and plasticity, and pliability in the African character. This softness may be collected almost every where from the Travels of Mr. Mungo Park, and has been noticed by other writers, who have contrasted it with the unbending ferocity of the North American Indians and other tribes. But if this be a feature in the African character, we may account for the uniformity of the conduct of those Africans, who were liberated on the several occasions above mentioned, or for their yielding so uniformly to the impressions, which had been given them by their superiors, after they had been made free; and, if this be so, why should not our colonial slaves, if emancipated, conduct themselves in the same manner? Besides, I am not sure whether the good conduct of the liberated in these cases was not to be attributed in part to a sense of interest, when they came to know, that their condition *was to be improved.* Self-interest is a leading principle with all who are born into the world; and why is the Negro slave in our colonies to be shut out from this common feeling of our nature?—why is he to rise against his master, when he is informed that his condition is to be bettered? Did not the planters, as I have before related, declare in the House of Commons in the year 1816, that their Negroes had then imbibed the idea that they were to be made free, and that they were *extremely restless on that account?* But what was the cause of all this restlessness? Why, undoubtedly the thought of their emancipation was so interesting, or rather a matter of such exceedingly great joy to them, that *they could not help thinking and talking of it.* And would not this be the case with our Negroes at this moment, if such a prospect were to be set before them? But if they would be overjoyed at this prospect, is it likely they would cut the throats of those, who should attempt to realize it? would they not, on the other hand, be disposed to conduct themselves equally well as the other African slaves before mentioned, when they came to know, that they were immediately to be prepared for the reception of this great blessing, the *first guarantee* of which would be an *immediate* and *living experience* of better laws and better treatment?

The fifth case may comprehend the slaves of St. Domingo as they were made free at different intervals in the course of the French Revolution.

To do justice to this case, I must give a history of the different circumstances connected with it. It may be remembered, then, that when the French Revolution, which decreed equality of rights to all citizens, had taken place, the *free People of Colour* of St. Domingo, many of whom were persons of large property and liberal education, petitioned the National Assembly, that they might enjoy the same political privileges as the *Whites* there. At length the subject of the petition was discussed, but not till the 8th of March 1790, when the Assembly agreed upon a decree concerning it. The decree, however, was worded so ambiguously, that the two parties in St. Domingo, the *Whites* and the *People of Colour,* interpreted it each of them in its own favour. This difference of interpretation gave rise to animosities between them, and these animosities were augmented by political party-spirit, according as they were royalists or partizans of the French Revolution, so that disturbances took place and blood was shed.

In the year 1791, the People of Colour petitioned the Assembly again, but principally for an explanation of the decree in question. On the 15th of May, the subject was taken into consideration, and the result was another decree in explicit terms, which determined, that the *People of Colour* in all the French islands were entitled to all the rights of citizenship, provided *they were born of free parents on both sides*. The news of this decree had no sooner arrived at the Cape, than it produced an indignation almost amounting to phrensy among the *Whites*. They directly trampled under foot the national cockade, and with difficulty were prevented from seizing all the French merchant ships in the roads. After this the two parties armed against each other. Even camps began to be formed. Horrible massacres and conflagrations followed, the reports of which, when brought to the mother-country, were so terrible, that the Assembly abolished the decree in favour of *the Free People of Colour* in the same year.

In the year 1792, the news of the rescinding of the decree as now stated, produced, when it reached St. Domingo, as much irritation among the People of Colour, as the news of the passing of it had done among the Whites, and hostilities were renewed between them, so that new battles, massacres, and burnings, took place. Suffice it to say, that as soon as these events became known in France, the Conventional Assembly, which had then succeeded the Legislative, took them into consideration. Seeing, however, nothing but difficulties and no hope of reconciliation on either side, they knew not what other course to take than to do justice, whatever the consequences might be. They resolved, accordingly, in the month of April, that the decree of 1791, which had been both made and reversed by the preceding Assembly in the same year, should stand good. They restored therefore the People of Colour to the privileges which had been before voted to them, and appointed Santhonax, Polverel, and another, to repair in person to St. Domingo, with a large body of troops, and to act there as commissioners, and, among other things, to enforce the decree and to keep the peace.

In the year 1793, the same divisions and the same bad blood continuing, notwithstanding the arrival of the commissioners, a very trivial matter, viz. a quarrel between a *Mulatto* and a *White man* (an officer in the French marine), gave rise to new disasters. This quarrel took place on the 20th of June. On the same day the seamen left their ships in the roads, and came on shore, and made common cause of the affair with the white inhabitants of the town. On the other side were opposed the Mulattos and other People of Colour, and these were afterwards joined by some insurgent Blacks. The battle lasted nearly two days. During this time the arsenal was taken and plundered, and some thousands were killed in the streets, and more than half the town was burnt. The commissioners, who were spectators of this horrible scene, and who had done all they could to restore peace, escaped unhurt, but they were left upon a heap of ruins, and with but little more power than the authority which their commission gave them. They had only about a thousand troops left in the place. They determined, therefore, under these circumstances, to call in the Negro Slaves in the neighbourhood to their assistance. They issued a proclamation in consequence, by which *they promised to give freedom to all the Blacks who were willing to range themselves under the banners of the Republic.* This was the first proclamation made by public authority for emancipating slaves in St. Domingo. It is usually called the Proclamation of Santhonax, though both commissioners had a hand in it; and sometimes, in allusion to the place where it was issued (the Cape), the Proclamation of the North. The result of it was, that a considerable number of slaves came in and were enfranchised.

Soon after this transaction Polverel left his colleague Santhonax at the Cape, and went in his capacity of commissioner to Port au Prince, the capital of the West. Here he found every thing quiet, and cultivation in a flourishing state. From Port au Prince he visited Les Cayes, the capital of the South. He had not, however, been long there, before he found that the minds of the slaves began to be in an unsettled state. They had become acquainted with what had taken place in the north, not only with the riots at the Cape, but the proclamation of Santhonax. Now this proclamation, though it sanctioned freedom only for a particular or temporary purpose, did not exclude it from any particular quarter. The terms therefore appeared to be open to all who would accept them. Polverel therefore, seeing the impression which it had begun to make upon the minds of the slaves in these parts, was convinced that emancipation could be neither stopped nor retarded, and that it was absolutely necessary for *the personal safety of the white planters,* that it should be extended *to the whole island.* He was so convinced of the necessity of this, *that he drew up a proclamation* without further delay *to that effect,* and *put it into circulation.* He dated it from Les Cayes. He exhorted the planters to patronize it. He advised them, if they wished to avoid the most serious calamities, to concur themselves in the proposition of giving freedom to their slaves. He then caused a register to be opened at the Government house to receive the signatures of all those who should approve of his advice. It was remarkable that all the proprietors in these parts inscribed their names in the book. He then caused a similar register to be opened at Port au Prince for the West. Here the same disposition was found to prevail. All the planters, except one, gave in their signatures. They had become pretty generally convinced by this time, that their own personal safety was connected with the measure. It may be proper to observe here, that the proclamation last mentioned, which preceded these registries, though it was the act of Polverel alone, was sanctioned afterwards by Santhonax. It is, however, usually called the Proclamation of Polverel or of Les Cayes. It came out in September 1793. We may now add, that in the month of February 1794, the Conventional Assembly of France, though probably ignorant of what the commissioners had now done, passed a decree for the abolition of slavery throughout *the whole of the French colonies*. Thus the Government of the mother-country, without knowing it, confirmed freedom to those upon whom it had been bestowed by the commissioners. This decree put therefore *the finishing stroke to the whole*. It completed the emancipation of the *whole slave population of St. Domingo*.

Having now given a concise history of the abolition of slavery in St. Domingo, I shall inquire how those who were liberated on these several occasions conducted themselves after this change in their situation. It is of great importance to us to know, whether they used their freedom properly, or whether they abused it.

With respect to those emancipated by Santhonax in the North, we have nothing to communicate. They were made free for military purposes only; and we have no clue whereby we can find out what became of them afterwards.

With respect to those who were emancipated next in the South, and those directly afterwards in the West, by the proclamation of Polverel, we are enabled to give a very pleasing account. Fortunately for our views, Colonel Malenfant, who was resident in the island at the time, has made us acquainted with their general conduct and character. His account, though short, is quite sufficient for our purpose. Indeed it is highly satisfactory[6]. "After this public act of emancipation," says he, (by Polverel,) "the Negroes *remained quiet* both *in the South and in the West*, and they *continued to work upon all the plantations*. There were estates, indeed, which had neither owners nor managers resident upon them, for some of these had been put into prison by Montbrun; and others, fearing the same fate, had fled to the quarter which had just been given up to the English. Yet upon these estates, though abandoned, the Negroes *continued their labours*, where there were any, even inferior, agents to guide them; and on those estates, where no white men were left to direct them, they betook themselves to the planting of provisions; but upon *all the plantations* where the Whites resided, the Blacks *continued to labour as quietly as before*." A little further on in the work, ridiculing the notion entertained in France, that the Negroes would not work without compulsion, he takes occasion to allude to other Negroes, who had been liberated by the same proclamation, but who were more immediately under his own eye and cognizance[7]. "If," says he, "you will take care not to speak to them of their return to slavery, but talk to them about their liberty, you may with this latter word chain them down to their labour. How did Toussaint succeed? How did I succeed also before his time in the plain of the Cul de Sac, and on the Plantation Gouraud, more than eight months after liberty had been granted (by Polverel) to the slaves? Let those who knew me at that time, and even the Blacks themselves, be asked. They will all reply, that *not a single Negro* upon that plantation, consisting of more than four hundred and fifty labourers, *refused to work*; and yet this plantation was thought to be under the worst discipline, and the slaves the most idle, of any in the plain. I, myself, inspired the same activity into three other plantations, of which I had the management."

The above account is far beyond any thing that could have been expected. Indeed, it is most gratifying. We find that the liberated Negroes, *both in the South and the West*, continued to work upon their *old plantations*, and for their *old masters*; that there was also *a spirit of industry* among them, and that they gave no uneasiness to their employers; for they are described as continuing to work *as quietly as before*. Such was the conduct of the Negroes for the first nine months after their liberation, or up to the middle of 1794. Let us pursue the subject, and see how they conducted themselves after this period.

During the year 1795 and part of 1796 I learn nothing about them, neither good, nor bad, nor indifferent, though I have ransacked the French historians for this purpose. Had there, however, been any thing in the way of *outrage*, I should have heard of it; and let me take this opportunity of setting my readers right, if, for want of knowing the dates of occurrences, they should have connected *certain outrages*, which assuredly took place in St. Domingo, *with the emancipation of the slaves*. The great massacres and conflagrations, which have made so frightful a picture in the history of this unhappy island, had been all effected *before the proclamations* of Santhonax and Polverel. They had all taken place *in the days of slavery*, or before the year 1794, that is, before the great conventional decree of the mother country was known. They had been occasioned, too, *not originally by the slaves themselves*, but by quarrels between *the white and coloured planters*, and between the *royalists* and the *revolutionists*, who, for the purpose of reeking their vengeance upon each other, called in the aid of their respective slaves; and as to the insurgent Negroes of the North, who filled that part of the colony so often with terror and dismay, they were originally put in motion, according to Malenfant, under *the auspices of the royalists* themselves, to strengthen their own cause, and *to put down the partizans of the French revolution*. When Jean François and Biassou commenced the insurrection, there were many *white royalists* with them, and the Negroes were made to wear the *white cockade*. I repeat, then, that during the years 1795 and 1796, I can find nothing in the History of St. Domingo, wherewith to reproach the emancipated Negroes in the way of outrage[8]. There is every reason, on the other hand, to believe, that they conducted themselves, during this period, in as orderly a manner as before.

I come now to the latter part of the year 1796; and here happily a clue is furnished me, by which I have an opportunity of pursuing my inquiry with pleasure. We shall find, that from this time there was no want of industry in those who had been emancipated, nor want of obedience in them as hired servants: they maintained, on the other hand, a respectable character. Let us appeal first to Malenfant. "The colony," says he[9], "was *flourishing under Toussaint. The Whites lived happily and in peace upon their estates, and the Negroes continued to work for them.*" Now Toussaint came into power, being general-in-chief of the armies of St. Domingo, a little before the end of the year 1796, and remained in power till the year 1802, or till the invasion of the island by the French expedition of Buonaparte under Leclerc. Malenfant means therefore to state, that from the latter end of 1796 to 1802, a period of six years, the planters or farmers kept possession of their estates; that they lived upon them, and that they lived upon them peaceably, that is, without interruption or disturbance from any one; and, finally, that the Negroes, though they had been all set free, continued to be their labourers. Can there be any account more favourable to our views than this, after so sudden an emancipation.

I may appeal next to General Lacroix, who published his "Memoirs for a History of St. Domingo," at Paris, in 1819. He informs us, that when Santhonax, who had been recalled to France by the Government there, returned to the colony in 1796, "*he was astonished at the state in which he found it on his return.*" This, says Lacroix[10], "was owing to Toussaint, who, while he had succeeded in establishing perfect order and discipline among the black troops, had succeeded also in making the black labourers return to the plantations, there to resume the drudgery of cultivation."

But the same author tells us, that in the next year (1797) the most wonderful progress had been made in agriculture. He uses these remarkable words: "*The colony,*" says he[11], "*marched, as by enchantment, towards its ancient splendour; cultivation prospered; every day produced perceptible proofs of its progress. The city of the Cape and the plantations of the North rose up again visibly to the eye.*" Now I am far from wishing to attribute all this wonderful improvement, this daily visible progress in agriculture, to the mere act of the emancipation of the slaves in St. Domingo. I know that many other circumstances which I could specify, if I had room, contributed towards its growth; but I must be allowed to maintain, that unless the Negroes, who were then free, *had done their part as labourers*, both by working regularly and industriously, and by obeying the directions of their superintendants or masters, the colony could never have gone on, as relates to cultivation, with the rapidity described.

The next witness to whom I shall appeal, is the estimable General Vincent, who lives now at Paris, though at an advanced age. Vincent was a colonel, and afterwards a general of brigade of artillery in St. Domingo. He was stationed there during the time both of Santhonax and Toussaint. He was also a proprietor of estates in the island. He was the man who planned the renovation of its agriculture after the abolition of slavery, and one of the great instruments in bringing it to the perfection mentioned by Lacroix. In the year 1801, he was called upon by Toussaint to repair to Paris, to lay before the Directory the new constitution, which had been agreed upon in St. Domingo. He obeyed the summons. It happened, that he arrived in France just at the moment of the peace of Amiens; here he found, to his inexpressible surprise and grief, that Buonaparte was preparing an immense armament, to be commanded by Leclerc, for the purpose of *restoring slavery in St. Domingo*. He lost no time in seeing the First Consul, and he had the courage to say at this interview what, perhaps, no other man in France would have dared to say at this particular moment. He remonstrated against the expedition; he told him to his face, that though the army destined for this purpose was composed of the brilliant conquerors of Europe, it could do nothing in the Antilles. It would most assuredly be destroyed by the climate of St. Domingo, even though it should be doubtful, whether it would not be destroyed by the Blacks. He stated, as another argument against the expedition, that it was totally unnecessary, and therefore criminal; for that every thing *was going on well* in St. Domingo. *The proprietors were in peaceable possession of their estates; cultivation was making a rapid progress; the Blacks were industrious, and beyond example happy.* He conjured him, therefore, in the name of humanity, not to reverse this beautiful state of things. But alas! his efforts were ineffectual. The die had been cast: and the only reward, which he received from Buonaparte for his manly and faithful representations, was banishment to the Isle of Elba.

Having carried my examination into the conduct of the Negroes after their liberation to 1802, or to the invasion of the island by Leclerc, I must now leave a blank for nearly two years, or till the year 1804. It cannot be expected during a war, in which every man was called to arms to defend his own personal liberty, and that of every individual of his family, that we should see plantations cultivated as quietly as before, or even cultivated at all. But this was not the fault of *the emancipated Negroes*, but of *their former masters*. It was owing to the prejudices of the latter, that this frightful invasion took place; prejudices, indeed, common to all planters, where slavery obtains, from the very nature of their situation, and upon which I have made my observations in a former place. Accustomed to the use of arbitrary power, they could no longer brook the loss of their whips. Accustomed again to look down upon the Negroes as an inferior race of beings, or as the reptiles of the earth, they could not bear, peaceably as these had conducted themselves, to come into that familiar contact with them, as *free labourers*, which the change of their situation required. They considered them, too, as property lost, but which was to be recovered. In an evil hour, they prevailed upon Buonaparte, by false representations and *promises of pecuniary support*, to restore things to their former state. The hellish expedition at length arrived upon the shores of St. Domingo:—a scene of blood and torture followed, *such as history had never before disclosed*, and compared with which, *though planned and executed by Whites[12]*, all the barbarities said to have been perpetrated by the *insurgent Blacks* of the North, *amount comparatively to nothing*. In fine, the French were driven from the island. Till that time, the planters retained their property, and then it was, but not till then, that they lost their all; it cannot, therefore, be expected, as I have said before, that I should have any thing to say in favour of the industry or good order of the emancipated Negroes, *during such a convulsive period*.

In the year 1804, Dessalines was proclaimed emperor of this fine territory. Here I resume the thread of my history, (though it will be but for a moment,) in order that I may follow it to its end. In process of time, the black troops, containing the Negroes in question, were disbanded, except such as were retained for the peace-establishment of the army. They, who were disbanded, returned to cultivation. As they were free when they became soldiers, so they continued to be free when they became labourers again. From that time to this, there has been no want of subordination or industry among them. They or their descendants are the persons, by whom the plains and valleys of St. Domingo *are still cultivated*, and they are reported to follow their occupations still, and with *as fair a character* as other free labourers in any other quarter of the globe.

We have now seen, that the emancipated Negroes never abused their liberty, from the year 1793 (the era of their general emancipation) to the present day, a period of *thirty* years. An important question then seems to force itself upon us, "What were the measures taken after so frightful an event, as that of emancipation, to secure the tranquillity and order which has been described, or to rescue the planters and the colony from ruin?" I am bound to answer this, if I can, were it only to gratify the curiosity of my readers; but more particularly when I consider, that if emancipation should ever be in contemplation in our own colonies, it will be desirable to have all the light possible upon that subject, and particularly of precedent or example. It appears then, that the two commissioners, Santhonax and Polverel, aware of the mischief which might attend their decrees, were obliged to take the best measures they could devise to prevent it. One of their first steps was to draw up a short code of rules to be observed upon the plantations. These rules were printed and made public. They were also ordered to be read aloud to all the Negroes upon every estate, for which purpose the latter were to be assembled at a particular hour once a week. The preamble to these regulations insisted upon *the necessity of working, without which everything would go to ruin.* Among the articles, the two the most worthy of our notice were, that the labourers were to be obliged to hire themselves to their masters for *not less than a year*, at the end of which (September), but not before, they might quit their service, and engage with others; and that they were to receive *a third part* of the produce of the estate, as a recompense for their labour. These two were *fundamental* articles. As to the minor, they were not alike upon every estate. This code of the commissioners subsisted for about three years.

Toussaint, when he came into power, reconsidered this subject, and adopted a code of rules of his own. His first object was to prevent oppression on the part of the master or employer, and yet to secure obedience on the part of the labourer. Conceiving that there could be no liberty where any one man had the power of punishing another at his discretion, he took away from every master the use of the whip, and of the chain, and of every other instrument of correction, either by himself or his own order: he took away, in fact, *all power of arbitrary punishment.* Every master offending against this regulation was to be summoned, on complaint by the labourer, before a magistrate or intendant of police, who was to examine into the case, and to act accordingly. Conceiving, on the other hand, that a just subordination ought to be kept up, and that, wherever delinquency occurred, punishment ought to follow, he ordained, that all labourers offending against the plantation laws, or not performing their contracts, should be brought before the same magistrate or intendant of police, who should examine them touching such delinquency, and decide as in the former case: thus he administered justice without respect of persons. It must be noticed, that all punishments were to be executed by a civil officer, a sort of public executioner, that they might be considered as punishments *by the state.* Thus he *kept up discipline* on the plantations, *without lessening authority* on the one hand, and *without invading the liberty of individuals* on the other.

Among his plantation offences was idleness on the part of the labourer. A man was not to receive wages from his master, and to do nothing. He was obliged to perform a reasonable quantity of work, or be punished. Another offence was absence without leave, which was considered as desertion.

Toussaint differed from the commissioners, as to the length of time for which labourers should engage themselves to masters. He thought it unwise to allow the former, in the infancy of their liberty, to get notions of change and rambling at the end of every year. He ordained, therefore, that they should be attached to the plantations, and made, though free labourers, a sort of *adscripti glebae* for five years.

He differed again from the commissioners, as to the quantum of compensation for their labour. He thought one-third of the produce too much, seeing that the planter had another third to pay to the Government. He ordered, therefore, one-fourth to the labourer, but this was in the case only, where the labourer clothed and maintained himself: where he did not do this, he was entitled to a fourth only nominally, for out of this his master was to make a deduction for board and clothing.

The above is all I have been able to collect of the code of Toussaint, which, under his auspices, had the surprising effect of preserving tranquillity and order, and of keeping up a spirit of industry on the plantations of St. Domingo, at a time when only idleness and anarchy were to have been expected. It was in force when Leclerc arrived with his invading army, and it continued in force when the French army were beaten and Negro-liberty confirmed. From Toussaint it passed to Dessalines, and from Dessalines to Christophe and Petion, and from the two latter to Boyer; and it is the code therefore which regulates, and I believe with but very little variation, the relative situation of master and servant in husbandry at this present hour.

But it is time that I should now wind up the case before us. And, first, will any one say that this case is not analogous to that which we have in contemplation? Let us remember that the number of slaves liberated by the French decrees in St. Domingo was very little short of 500,000 persons, and that this was nearly equal to the number *of all the slaves* then in the British West Indian Islands when put together. But if there be a want of analogy, the difference lies on my side of the question. I maintain, that emancipation in *St. Domingo* was attended with *far more hazard* to persons and property, and with *far greater difficulties*, than it could possibly be, if attempted *in our own islands*. Can we forget that by the decree of Polverel, sanctioned afterwards by the Convention, all the slaves *were made free at once*, or *in a single day*? No notice was given of the event, and of course *no preparation* could be made for it. They were released *suddenly* from *all their former obligations and restraints*. They were let loose upon the Whites, their masters, with *all the vices of slavery* upon them. What was to have been expected but the dissolution of all civilized society, with the reign of barbarism and terror? Now all I ask for with respect to the slaves in our own islands is, that they should be emancipated *by degrees*, or that they should be made to pass through a certain course of discipline, *as through a preparatory school*, to fit them for the right use of their freedom. Again, can we forget the unfavourable circumstances, in which the slaves of St. Domingo were placed, for a year or two before their liberation, in another point of view? The island at this juncture was a prey to *political discord, civil war*, and *foreign invasion*, at the same time. Their masters were politically at variance with each other, as they were white or coloured persons, or republicans or royalists. They were quarrelling and fighting with each other, and shedding each other's blood. The English, who were in possession of the strong maritime posts, were alarming the country by their incursions: they, the slaves, had been trained up to the same political animosities. They had been made to take the side of their respective masters, and to pass through scenes of violence and bloodshed. Now, whenever emancipation is to be proposed in our own colonies, I anticipate neither *political parties*, nor *civil wars*, nor *foreign invasion*, but a time of *tranquillity and peace*. Who then will be bold enough to say, after these remarks, that there could be any thing like the danger and difficulties in emancipating the slaves there, which existed when the slaves of St. Domingo were made free? But some objector may say, after all, "There is one point in which your analogy is deficient. While Toussaint was in power, the Government of St. Domingo was a *black* one, and the Blacks would be more willing to submit to the authority of a *black* (their own) Government, than of a *white one*. Hence there Were less disorders after emancipation in St. Domingo, than would have probably occurred, had it been tried in our own islands." But to such an objector I should reply, that he knows nothing of the history of St. Domingo. The Government of that island was French, or *white*, from the very infancy of emancipation to the arrival of the expedition of Leclerc. The slaves were made free under the government of Santhonax and Polverel. When these retired, other *white* commissioners succeeded them. When Toussaint came into power, he was not supreme; Generals Hedouille, Vincent, and others, had a share in the government. Toussaint himself *received his commission from the French Directory*, and acted under it. He caused it every where to be made known, but particularly among his officers and troops, that he retained the island for the *French Government*, and that *France* was the *mother-country*.

A sixth class of slaves emancipated in bodies may comprehend those, who began to be liberated about eighteen months ago in the newly-erected State of Columbia. General Bolivar began the great work himself by enfranchising his own slaves, to the number of between seven and eight hundred. But he was not satisfied with this; for believing, as he did, that to hold persons in slavery at all, was not only morally wrong, but utterly inconsistent with the character of men fighting for their own liberty, he brought the subject before the Congress of Venezuela. The Congress there, after having duly considered it, drew up resolutions accordingly, which it recommended to the first general Congress of Columbia, when it should be assembled. This last congress, which met at the time expected, passed a decree for emancipation on the 19th of July 1821. All slaves, who had assisted, in a military capacity, in achieving the independence of the republic, were at once declared free. All the children of slaves, born after the said 19th of July, were to be free in succession as they attained the eighteenth year of their age. A fund was established at the same time by a general tax upon property, to pay the owners of such young slaves the expense of bringing them up to their eighteenth year, and for putting them afterwards to trades and useful professions; and the same fund was made applicable to the purchase of the freedom of adults in each district every year, during the three national festivals in December, as far as the district-funds would permit. Care, however, was to be taken to select those of the best character. It may be proper to observe, that emancipation, as above explained, has been proceeding regularly, from the 19th of July 1821, according to the terms of the decree, and also according to the ancient Spanish code, which still exists, and which is made to go hand in hand with it. They who attain their eighteenth year are not allowed to go at large after their liberation, but are put under the charge of special juntas for a useful education. The adults may have land, if they desire it, or they may go where they please. The State has lately purchased freedom for many of the latter, who had a liking to the army. Their freedom is secured to them whether they remain soldiers or are discharged. It is particularly agreeable to me to be able to say that all, who have been hitherto emancipated, have conducted themselves since that time with propriety. It appears by a letter from Columbia, dated 17th February 1822, about seven months after emancipation had commenced, addressed to James Stephen, Esq. of London, and since made public, "that the slaves were all then *peaceably at work* throughout the republic, as well as *the newly enfranchised* and those originally free." And it appears from the account of a gentleman of high consideration just arrived from Columbia, in London, that up to the time of his departure, they who had been emancipated "were *steady* and *industrious*, and that they *had conducted themselves well without a single exception.*" But as this is an experiment which it will yet take sixteen years to complete, it can only be called to our aid, as far as the result of it is known. It is, however, an experiment to which, as far as it has been made, we may appeal with satisfaction: for when we consider that *eighteen* months have elapsed, and that *many[13] thousands* have been freed since the passing of the decree and the date of the last accounts from Columbia, the decree cannot but be considered to have had a sufficient trial.

The seventh class may comprehend the slaves of the Honourable Joshua Steele, whose emancipation was attempted in Barbadoes between the years 1783 and 1790.

It appears that Mr. Steele lived several years in London. He was Vice-president of the London Society of Arts, Manufactures, and Commerce, and a person of talent and erudition. He was the proprietor of three estates in Barbadoes. His agent there used to send him accounts annually of his concerns; but these were latterly so ruinous, not only in a pecuniary point of view, but as they related to what Mr. Steele called the *destruction* of his Negroes, that he resolved, though then at the advanced age of eighty, to go there, and to look into his affairs himself. Accordingly he embarked, and arrived there early in the year 1780.

Mr. Steele had not been long in Barbadoes, before he saw enough to convince him that there was something radically wrong in the management of the slaves there, and he was anxious to try, as well for the sake of humanity as of his own interest, to effect a change in it. But how was he to accomplish this[14]? "He considered within himself how difficult it would be, nay, impossible, for a single proprietor to attempt so great a novelty as to bring about an alteration of manners and customs protected by iniquitous laws, and to which the gentlemen of the country were reconciled as to the best possible for amending the indocile and intractable ignorance of Negro slaves." It struck him however, among the expedients which occurred, that he might be able to form a Society, similar to the one in London, for the purpose of improving the arts, manufactures, and commerce of Barbadoes; and if so, he "indulged a hope that by means of it conferences might be introduced on patriotic subjects, in the course of which new ideas and new opinions might soften the national bigotry, so far as to admit some discourses on the possibility of amendment in the mode of governing slaves." Following up this idea, he brought it at length to bear. A Society was formed, in consequence, of gentlemen of the island in 1781. The subjects under its discussion became popular. It printed its first minutes in 1782, which were very favourably received, and it seemed to bid fair after this to answer the benevolent views of its founder.

During this time, a space of two years, Mr. Steele had been gaining a practical knowledge of the West Indian husbandry, and also a practical knowledge of the temper, disposition, habits, and customs of the slaves. He had also read much and thought much. It may be inferred from his writings, that three questions especially had employed his mind. 1. Whether he could not do away all arbitrary punishments and yet keep up discipline among the slaves? 2. Whether he could not carry on the plantation-work through the stimulus of reward? 3. Whether he could not change slavery into a condition of a milder name and character, so that the slaves should be led by degrees to the threshold of liberty, from whence they might step next, without hazard, into the rank of free men, if circumstances should permit and encourage such a procedure. Mr. Steele thought, after mature consideration, that he could accomplish all these objects, and he resolved to make the experiments gradually upon his own estates.

At the end of the year 1783 he put the first of these questions to trial. "I took," says he, "the whips and all power of arbitrary punishment from all the overseers and their white servants, which occasioned *my chief overseer to resign,* and I soon dismissed all his deputies, who *could not bear the loss of their whips;* but at the same time, that a proper subordination and obedience to lawful orders and duty should be preserved, I created a *magistracy out of the Negroes* themselves, and appointed a court or jury of the elder Negroes or head-men for trial and punishment of all casual offences, (and these courts were always to be held in my presence, or in that of my new superintendant,) which court *very soon grew respectable.* Seven of these men being of the rank of drivers in their different departments, were also constituted *rulers*, as magistrates over all the gang, and were charged to see at all times that nothing should go wrong in the plantations; but that on all necessary occasions they should assemble and consult together how any such wrong should be immediately rectified; and I made it known to all the gangs, that the authority of these rulers should supply the absence or vacancy of an overseer in all cases; they making daily or occasional reports of all occurrences to the proprietor or his delegate for his approbation or his orders."

It appears that Mr. Steele was satisfied with this his first step, and he took no other for some time. At length, in about another year, he ventured upon the second. He "tried whether he could not obtain the labour of his Negroes by *voluntary* means instead of the old method by violence." On a certain day he offered a pecuniary reward for holing canes, which is the most laborious operation in West Indian husbandry. "He offered two-pence half-penny (currency), or about three-halfpence (sterling), per day, with the usual allowance to holers of a dram with molasses, to any twenty-five of his Negroes, both men and women, who would undertake to hole for canes an acre per day, at about 96-1/2 holes for each Negro to the acre. The whole gang were ready to undertake it; but only fifty of the volunteers were accepted, and many among them were those who *on much lighter occasions* had usually pleaded *infirmity and inability*: but the ground having been moist, they holed twelve acres within six days with great ease, having had *an hour*, more or less, *every evening to spare*, and the like experiment was repeated with the like success. More experiments with such premiums on weeding and deep hoeing were made by task-work per acre, and all succeeded in like manner, their premiums being all punctually paid them in proportion to their performance. But afterwards some of the same people being put *without premium* to weed on a loose cultivated soil in the common manner, *eighteen* Negroes did not do as much in a given time as *six* had performed of the like sort of work a few days before with the premium of two-pence half-penny." The next year Mr. Steele made similar experiments. Success attended him again; and from this time task-work, or the *voluntary* system, became the general practice of the estate. Mr. Steele did not proceed to put the third question to trial till the year 1789. The Society of Arts, which he had instituted in 1781, had greatly disappointed him. Some of the members, looking back to the discussions which had taken place on the subject of Slavery, began to think that they had gone too far as slaveholders in their admissions. They began to insinuate, "that they had been taken in, under the specious appearance of promoting the arts, manufactures, and commerce of Barbadoes, *to promote dangerous designs against its established laws and customs.*" Discussions therefore of this sort became too unpopular to be continued. It was therefore not till Mr. Steele found, that he had no hope of assistance from this Society, and that he was obliged to depend solely upon himself, that he put in force the remainder of his general plan. He had already (in 1783), as we stated some time ago, abolished arbitrary punishment and instituted a Negro-magistracy; and since that time (in 1785) he had adopted the system of *working by the piece*. But the remaining part of his plan went the length of *altering the condition* of the slaves themselves; and it is of this alteration, a most important one (in 1789), that I am now to speak.

Mr. Steele took the hint for the particular mode of improving the condition of his slaves, which I am going to describe, from the practice of our Anglo-Saxon ancestors in the days of Villainage, which, he says, was "the most wise and excellent mode of civilizing savage slaves." There were in those days three classes of villains. The first or lowest consisted of villains in gross, who were alienable at pleasure. The second of villains regardent, who were *adscripti glebae*, or attached as freehold property to the soil. And the third or last of copyhold bondmen, who had tenements of land, for which they were bound to pay in services. The villains first mentioned, or those of the lowest class, had all these gradations to pass through, from the first into the second, and from the second into the third, before they could become free men. This was the model, from which Mr. Steele resolved to borrow, when he formed his plan for changing the condition of his slaves. Me did not, however, adopt it throughout, but he chose out of it what he thought would be most suitable to his purpose, and left the rest. We may now see what the plan was, when put together, from the following account.

In the year 1789 he erected his plantations into *manors*. It appears that the Governor of Barbadoes had the power by charter, with the consent of the majority of the council, of dividing the island into manors, lordships, and precincts, and of making freeholders; and though this had not yet been done, Mr. Steele hoped, as a member of council, to have influence sufficient to get his own practice legalized in time. Presuming upon this, he registered in the *manor*-book all his adult male slaves as *copyholders*. He then gave to these separate tenements of lands, which they were to occupy, and upon which they were to raise whatever they might think most advantageous to their support. These tenements consisted of half an acre of plantable and productive land to each adult, a quantity supposed to be sufficient with industry to furnish him and his family with provision and clothing. The tenements were made descendible to the heirs of the occupiers or copyholders, that is, to their children *on the plantations*; for no part of the succession was to go out of the plantations to the issue of any foreign wife, and, in case of no such heir, they were to fall in to the lord to be re-granted according to his discretion. It was also inscribed that any one of the copyholders, who would not perform his services to the manor (the refractory and others), was to forfeit his tenement and his privileged rank, and to go back to villain in gross and to be subject to corporal punishment as before. "Thus," says Mr. Steele, "we run no risk whatever in making the experiment by giving such copyhold-tenements to all our well-deserving Negroes, and to all in general, when they appear to be worthy of that favour."

Matters having been adjusted so far, Mr. Steele introduced the practice of *rent* and *wages*. He put an annual rent upon each tenement, which he valued at so many days' labour. He set a rent also upon personal service, as due by the copyholder to his master in his former quality of slave, seeing that his master or predecessor had purchased a property in him, and this be valued in the same manner. He then added the two rents together, making so many days' work altogether, and estimated them in the current money of the time. Having done this, he fixed a daily wages or pay to be received by the copyholders for the work which they were to do. They were to work 260 days in the year for him, and to have 48 besides Sundays for themselves. He reduced these days' work also to current money. These wages he fixed at such a rate, that "they should be more than equivalent to the rent of their copyholds and the rent of their personal services when put together, in order to hold out to them an evident and profitable incentive to their industry." It appears that the rent of the tenement, half an acre, was fixed at the rate of 9*l.* currency, or between forty and fifty shillings sterling per acre, and the wages for a man belonging to the first gang at 7-1/2*d.* currency or 6*d.* sterling per day. As to the rent for the personal services, it is not mentioned.

With respect to labour and things connected with it, Mr. Steele entered the following among the local laws in the *court-roll* of the tenants and tenements. The copyholders were not to work for other masters without the leave of the lord. They were to work ten hours per day. If they worked over and above that time, they were to be paid for every hour a tenth part of their daily wages, and they were also to forfeit a tenth for every hour they were absent or deficient in the work of the day. All sorts of work, however, were to be reduced, as far as it could be done by observation and estimation, to equitable task-work. Hoes were to be furnished to the copyholders in the first instance; but they were to renew them, when worn out, at their own expense. The other tools were to be lent them, but to be returned to the storekeeper at night, or to be paid for in default of so doing. Mr. Steele was to continue the hospital and medical attendance at his own expense as before.

Mr. Steele, having now rent to receive and wages to pay, was obliged to settle a new mode of accounting between the plantation and the labourers. "He brought, therefore, all the minor crops of the plantation, such as corn, grain of all sorts, yams, eddoes, besides rum and molasses, into a regular cash account by weight and measure, which he charged to the copyhold-storekeeper at market prices of the current time, and the storekeeper paid them at the same prices to such of the copyholders as called for them in part of wages, in whose option it was to take either cash or goods, according to their earnings, to answer all their wants. Rice, salt, salt fish, barrelled pork, Cork butter, flour, bread, biscuit, candles, tobacco and pipes, and all species of clothing, were provided and furnished from the store at the lowest market prices. An account of what was paid for daily subsistence, and of what stood in their arrears to answer the rents of their lands, the fines and forfeitures for delinquencies, their head-levy and all other casual demands, was accurately kept in columns with great simplicity, and in books, which checked each other."

Such was the plan of Mr. Steele, and I have the pleasure of being able to announce, that the result of it was *highly satisfactory to himself*. In the year 1788, when only the first and second part of it had been reduced to practice, he spoke of it thus:—"A plantation," says he, "of between seven and eight hundred acres has been governed by fixed laws and a Negro-court *for about five years with great success*. In this plantation no overseer or white servant is allowed to lift his hand against a Negro, nor can he arbitrarily order a punishment. Fixed laws and a court or jury of their peers *keep all in order* without the ill effect of sudden and intemperate passions." And in the year 1790, about a year after the last part of his plan had been put to trial, he says in a letter to Dr. Dickson, "My copyholders have succeeded beyond my expectation." This was his last letter to that gentleman, for he died in the beginning of the next year. Mr. Steele went over to Barbadoes, as I have said before, in the year 1780, and he was then in the eightieth year of his age. He began his humane and glorious work in 1783, and he finished it in 1789. It took him, therefore, six years to bring his Negroes to the state of vassalage described, or to that state from whence he was sure that they might be transferred without danger in no distant time, to the rank of freemen, if it should be thought desirable. He lived one year afterwards to witness the success of his labours. He had accomplished, therefore, all he wished, and he died in the year 1791, in the ninety-first year of his age.

It may be proper now, and indeed useful to the cause which I advocate, to stop for a moment, just to observe the similarity of sentiment of two great men, quite unknown to each other; one of whom (Mr. Steele) was concerned in preparing Negro-slaves for freedom, and the other (Toussaint) in devising the best mode of managing them after they had been suddenly made free.

It appears, first, that they were both agreed in this point, viz. that the *first step* to be taken in either case, was *the total abolition of arbitrary punishment*.

It appears, secondly, that they were nevertheless both agreed again as to the necessity of punishing delinquents, but that they adopted different ways of bringing them to justice. Toussaint referred them to *magistrates*, but Mr. Steele *to a Negro-court*. I should prefer the latter expedient; first, because a Negro-court may be always at hand, whereas magistrates may live at a distance from the plantations, and not be always at home. Secondly, because the holding of a Negro-court would give consequence to those Negroes who should compose it, not only in their own eyes but in the eyes of others; and every thing, that might elevate the Black character, would be useful to those who were *on the road to emancipation*; and, lastly, because there must be some thing satisfactory and consoling to the accused to be tried by their peers.

It appears, thirdly, that both of them were agreed again in the principle of making the Negroes, in either case, *adscripti glebae*; or attached to the soil, though they might differ as to the length of time of such ascription.

And it appears, lastly, that they were agreed in another, and this the only remaining point, viz. on the necessity of holding out a stimulus to either, so as to excite in them a very superior spirit of industry to any they had known before. They resorted, however to different means to effect this. Toussaint gave the labourers one *fourth* of the produce of the land; deducting board and clothing. Mr. Steele, on the other hand, gave them *daily wages*. I do not know which to prefer; but the plan of Mr. Steele is most consonant to the English practice.

But to return. It is possible that some objector may rise up here as before, and say that even the case, which I have now detailed, is not, strictly speaking, analogous to that which we have in contemplation, and may argue thus:— "The case of Mr. Steele is not a complete precedent, because his slaves were never *fully* emancipated. He had brought them only to *the threshold* of liberty, but no further. They were only *copyholders*, but *not free men*." To this I reply, first, That Mr. Steele *accomplished all that he ever aimed at*. I have his own words for saying, that so long as the present iniquitous slave-laws, and the distinction of colour, should exist, it would be imprudent to go further. I reply again, That the partisans of emancipation would be happy indeed, if they could see the day when our West Indian slaves should arrive at the rank and condition of the copyholders of Mr. Steele. They wish for no other freedom than that which is *compatible with the joint interest of the master and the slave*. At the same time they must maintain, that the copyholders of Mr. Steele had been brought so near to the condition of free men, that a removal from one into the other, after a certain time, seemed more like a thing of course than a matter to be attended either with difficulty or danger: for unquestionably their moral character must have been improved. If they had ceased for seven years to feel themselves degraded by arbitrary punishment, they must have acquired some little independence of mind. If they had been paid for their labour, they must have acquired something like a spirit of industry. If they had been made to pay rent for their cottage and land, and to maintain themselves, they must have been made to *look beforehand*, to *think for themselves and families from day to day*, and to *provide against the future*, all which operations of the mind are the characteristics only of free men. The case, therefore, of Mr. Steele is most important and precious: for it shows us, first, that the emancipation, which we seek, is a thing which *may be effected.* The plan of Mr. Steele was put in force in *a British* Island, and that, which was done in one British Island, may under similar circumstances *be done again in the same, as well as in another.* It shows us, again, *how* this emancipation may be brought about. The process is so clearly detailed, that any one may follow it. It is also a case for encouragement, inasmuch as it was attended with success.

I have now considered no less than six cases of slaves emancipated in bodies, and a seventh of slaves, who were led up to the very threshold of freedom, comprehending altogether not less than between five and six hundred thousand persons; and I have considered also all the objections that could be reasonably advanced against them. The result is a belief on my part, that emancipation is not only *practicable*, but that it is *practicable without danger.* The slaves, whose cases I have been considering, were resident in different parts of the world. There must have been, amongst such a vast number, persons of *all characters.* Some were liberated, who had been *accustomed to the use of arms.* Others at a time when the land in which they sojourned was afflicted *with civil and foreign wars*; others again *suddenly*, and with *all the vicious habits of slavery upon them.* And yet, under all these disadvantageous circumstances, I find them all, without exception, *yielding themselves to the will of their superiors*, so as to be brought by them *with as much ease and certainty into the form intended for them*, as clay in the hands of the potter is fashioned to his own model. But, if this be so, I think I should be chargeable with a want of common sense, were I *to doubt for a moment*, that emancipation *was not practicable*; and I am not sure that I should not be exposed to the same charge, were I to doubt, that emancipation *was practicable without danger.* For I have not been able to discover (and it is most remarkable) *a single failure* in any of the cases which have been produced. I have not been able to discover throughout this vast mass of emancipated persons *a single instance of bad behaviour* on their parts, not even of a refusal to work, or of disobedience to orders. Much less have I seen frightful commotions, or massacres, or a return of evil for evil, or revenge for past injuries, even when they had it amply in their power. In fact, the Negro character is malleable at the European will. There is, as I have observed before, a singular pliability in the constitutional temper of the Negroes, and they have besides a quick sense of their own interest, which influences their conduct. I am convinced, that West India masters can do what they will with their slaves; and that they may lead them through any changes they please, and with perfect safety to themselves, if they will only make them (the slaves) understand that they are to be benefited thereby.

Having now established, I hope, two of my points, first, that emancipation is *practicable*, and, secondly, that it is *practicable without danger*, I proceed to show the probability that *it would be attended with profit* to those planters who should be permitted to adopt it. I return, therefore, to the case of Mr. Steele. I give him the prior hearing on this new occasion, because I am sure that my readers will be anxious to learn something more about him; or to know what became of his plans, or how far such humane endeavours were attended with success. I shall begin by quoting the following expressions of Mr. Steele. "I have employed and amused myself," says he, "by introducing *an entire new mode* of governing my own slaves, for their happiness, and also *for my own profit.*" It appears, then, that Mr. Steele's new method of management was *profitable.* Let us now try to make out from his own account, of what these profits consisted.

Mr. Steele informs us, that his superintendant had obliged him to hire all his holing at 3*l.* currency, or 2*l.* 2*s.* 10*d.* sterling per acre. He was very much displeased at these repeated charges; and then it was, that he put his second question to trial, as I have before related, viz. whether he could not obtain the labour of his Negroes by voluntary means, instead of by the old method by violence. He made, therefore, an attempt to introduce task-work, or labour with an expected premium for extraordinary efforts, upon his estates. He gave his Negroes therefore a small pecuniary reward over and above the usual allowances, and the consequence was, as he himself says, that "the *poorest, feeblest,* and by character *the most indolent* Negroes of the whole gang, cheerfully performed the holing of his land, generally said to be the most laborious work, for *less than a fourth part* of the stated price paid to the undertakers for holing." This experiment I have detailed in another place. After this he continued the practice of task-work or premium. He describes the operation of such a system upon the minds of his Negroes in the following words: "According to the vulgar mode of governing Negro-slaves, they feel only the desponding fear of punishment for doing less than they ought, without being sensible that the settled allowance of food and clothing is given, and should be accepted, as a reward for doing well, while in task-work the expectation of winning the reward, and the fear of losing it, have a double operation to exert their endeavours." Mr. Steele was also benefited again in another point of view by the new practice which he had introduced. "He was clearly convinced, that saving time, by doing in one day as much as would otherwise require three days, was *worth more than double the premium,* the *timely effects* on vegetation *being critical.*" He found also to his satisfaction, that "during all the operations under the premium there were *no disorders, no crowding to the sick-house,* as before."

I have now to make my remarks upon this account. It shows us clearly how Mr. Steele made a part of his profits. These profits consisted first of a *saving of expense* in his husbandry, which saving *was not made by others.* He had his land holed *at one-fourth* of the usual rate. Let us apply this to all the other operations of husbandry, such as weeding, deep hoeing, &c. in a large farm of nearly eight hundred acres, like his, and we shall see how considerable the savings would be in one year. His Negroes again did not counterfeit sickness as before, in order to be excused from labour, but rather wished to labour in order to obtain the reward. There was therefore no crowding to the hospitals. This constituted a *second source of saving*; for they who were in the hospitals were maintained by Mr. Steele without earning any thing, while they who were working in the field left to their master in their work, when they went home at night, a value equal at least to that which they had received from him for their day's labour. But there was another saving of equal importance, which Mr. Steele calls a saving of *time*, but which he might with more propriety have called a saving of *season*. This saving of season, he says, was worth *more than double the premium*; and so it might easily have been. There are soils, every farmer knows, which are so constituted, that if you miss your day, you miss your season; and, if you miss your season, you lose probably half your crop. The saving, therefore, of the season, by having a whole crop instead of half an one, was *a third source of saving of money*. Now let us put all these savings together, and they will constitute a great saving or profit; for as these savings were made by Mr. Steele in consequence of *his new plan*, and *were therefore not made by others*, they constituted an *extraordinary* profit to him; or they added to the profit, whatever it might have been, which he used to receive from the estate before his new plan was put in execution.

But I discover other ways in which Mr. Steele was benefited, as I advance in the perusal of his writings. It was impossible to overlook the following passage: "Now," says he (alluding to his new system), "every species of provisions raised on the plantations, or bought from the merchants, is charged at the market-price to the copyhold-store, and discharged by what has been paid on the several accounts of every individual bond-slave; whereas for all those species heretofore, I never saw in any plantation-book of my estates any account of what became of them, or how they were disposed of, nor of their value, other than in these concise words, *they were given in allowance to the Negroes and stock*. Every year, for six years past, this great plantation has bought several hundred bushels of corn, and was scanty in all ground-provisions, our produce always falling short. This year, 1790, *since the establishment of copyholders, though several less acres were planted* last year in Guinea corn than usual, yet we have been able to sell *several hundred bushels* at a high price, and *we have still a great stock in hand*. I can place this saving to no other account, than that there is now an exact account kept by all produce being paid as cash to the bond-slaves; and also as all our watchmen are obliged to pay for all losses that happen on their watch, they have found it their interest to look well to their charge; and consequently that we have had much less stolen from us than before this new government took place."

Here then we have seen *another considerable source of saving* to Mr. Steele, viz. that *he was not obliged to purchase any corn for his slaves as formerly.* My readers will be able to judge better of this saving, when I inform them of what has been the wretched policy of many of our planters in this department of their concerns. Look over their farming memoranda, and you will see *sugar, sugar, sugar,* in every page; but you may turn over leaf after leaf, before you will find the words *provision ground* for their slaves. By means of this wretched policy, slaves have often suffered most grievously. Some of them have been half-starved. Starvation, too, has brought on disorders which have ultimately terminated in their death. Hence their masters have suffered losses, besides the expense incurred in buying what they ought to have raised upon their own estates, and this perhaps at a dear market: and in this wretched predicament Mr. Steele appears to have been himself when he first went to the estate. His slaves, he tells us, had been reduced in number by bad management. Even for six years afterwards he had been obliged to buy several hundred bushels of corn; but in the year 1790 he had sold several hundred bushels at a high price, and had still a great stock on hand. And to what was all this owing? Not to an exact account kept at the store (for some may have so misunderstood Mr. Steele); for how could an exact account kept there, have occasioned an increase in the produce of the earth? but, as Mr. Steele himself says, *to the establishment of his copyholders*, or to the *alteration of the condition* of his slaves. His slaves did not only three times more work than before, in consequence of the superior industry he had excited among them, but, by so doing, they were enabled to put the corn into the earth three times more quickly than before, or they were so much forwarder in their other work, that they were enabled to sow it at the critical moment, or so as *to save the season*, and thus secure a full crop, or a larger crop on a less number of acres, than was before raised upon a greater. The copyholders, therefore, were the persons who increased the produce of the earth; but the exact account kept at the store prevented the produce from being misapplied as formerly. It could no longer be put down in the general expression of "given in allowances to the Negroes and the stock;" but it was put down to the copyholder, and to him only, who received it. Thus Mr. Steele saved the purchase of a great part of the provisions for his slaves. He had formerly a great deal to buy for them, but now nothing. On the other hand, he had to sell; but, as his slaves were made, according to the new system, to *maintain themselves*, he had now *the whole produce of his estate to dispose of.* The circumstance therefore of having nothing to buy, but every thing to sell, constituted another source of his profits.

What the other particular profits of Mr. Steele were I can no where find, neither can I find what were his particular expenses; so as to be enabled to strike the balance in his favour. Happily, however, Mr. Steele has done this for us himself, though he has not furnished us with the items on either side.—He says that "from the year 1773 to 1779 (he arrived in Barbadoes in 1780), his stock had been so much reduced by ill management and wasteful economy, that the annual average neat clearance was little more than *one and a quarter* per cent. on the purchase. In a second period of four years, in consequence of the exertion of an honest and able manager, (though with a further reduction of the stock, and including the loss from the great hurricane,) the annual average income was brought to clear *a little above two* per cent.; but in a third period of three years from 1784 to 1786 inclusive, *since the new mode of governing the Negroes,* (besides increasing the stock, and laying out large sums annually in adding necessary works, and in repairs of the damages by the great hurricane,) the estate has cleared very nearly *four and a quarter* per cent.; that is, its annual average clearance in each of these three periods, was in this proportion; for every 100*l.* annually cleared in the first period the annual average clearance in the second period was 158*l.* 10*s.*, and in the third period was 345*l.* 6*s.* 8*d.*" This is the statement given by Mr. Steele, and a most important one it is; for if we compare what the estate had cleared in the first, with what it had cleared in the last of these periods, and have recourse to figures, we shall find that Mr. Steele had *more than tripled* the income of it, in consequence of *his new management*, during his residence in Barbadoes. And this is in fact what he says himself in words at full length, in his answer to the 17th question proposed to him by the committee of the Privy-council on the affairs of the slave trade. "In a plantation," says he, "of 200 slaves in June 1780, consisting of 90 men, 82 women, 56 boys, and 60 girls, though under the exertions of an able and honest manager, there were only 15 births, and no less than 57 deaths, in three years and three months. An alteration was made in the mode of governing the slaves. The whips were taken from all the white servants. All arbitrary punishments were abolished, and all offences were tried and sentence passed by a Negro court. In four years and three months after this change of government, there were 44 births, and only 41 deaths, of which ten deaths were of superannuated men and women, some above 80 years old. But in the same interval the annual neat clearance of the estate was *above three times more than it had been for ten years before!!!*"

Dr. Dickson, the editor of Mr. Steele, mentions these profits also, and in the same terms, and connects them with an eulogium on Mr. Steele, which is worthy of our attention. "Mr. Steele," says he, "saw that the Negroes, like all other human beings, were to be stimulated to permanent exertion only by a sense of their own interests in providing for their own wants and those of their offspring. He therefore tried *rewards*, which immediately roused the most indolent to exertion. His experiments ended in *regular wages*, which the industry he had excited among his whole gang enabled him to pay. Here was a natural, efficient, and profitable reciprocity of interests. His people became contented; his mind was freed from that perpetual vexation and that load of anxiety, which are inseparable from the vulgar system, and in little more than four years the annual neat clearance of his property *was more than tripled*." Again, in another part of the work, "Mr. Steele's plan may no doubt receive some improvements, which his great age obliged him to decline"—"but it is perfect, as far as it goes. *To advance above 300 field-negroes, who had never before moved without the whip, to a state nearly resembling that of contented, honest and industrious servants, and, after paying for their labour, to triple in a few years the annual neat clearance of the estate,*—these, I say, were great achievements for an aged man in an untried field of improvement, pre-occupied by inveterate vulgar prejudice. He has indeed accomplished all that was really doubtful or difficult in the undertaking, and perhaps all that is at present desirable either for owner or slave; for he has ascertained as a fact, what was before only known to the learned as a theory, and to practical men as a paradox, that *the paying of slaves for their labour does actually produce a very great profit to their owners.*"

I have now proved (*as far as the plan[15] of Mr. Steele is concerned*) my third proposition, or *the probability that emancipation would promote the interests of those who should adopt it*; but as I know of no other estate similarly circumstanced with that of Mr. Steele, that is, where emancipation has been tried, and where a detailed result of it has been made known, I cannot confirm it by other similar examples. I must have recourse therefore to some new species of proof. Now it is an old maxim, as old as the days of Pliny and Columella, and confirmed by Dr. Adam Smith, and all the modern writers on political economy, that *the labour of free men is cheaper than the labour of slaves*. If therefore I should be able to show that this maxim would be true, if applied to all the operations and demands of West Indian agriculture, I should be able to establish my proposition on a new ground: for it requires no great acuteness to infer, that, if it be cheaper to employ free men than slaves in the cultivation of our islands, emancipation would be a profitable undertaking there.

I shall show, then, that the old maxim just mentioned is true, when applied to the case in our own islands, first, by establishing the fact, that *free men*, people of colour, in the East Indies, are employed in *precisely the same concerns* (the cultivation of the cane and the making of sugar) as the slaves in the West, and that they are employed *at a cheaper rate*. The testimony of Henry Botham, Esq. will be quite sufficient for this point. That gentleman resided for some time in the East Indies, where he became acquainted with the business of a sugar estate. In the year 1770 he quitted the East for the West. His object was to settle in the latter part of the world, if it should be found desirable so to do. For this purpose he visited all the West Indian islands, both English and French, in about two years. He became during this time a planter, though he did not continue long in this situation; and he superintended also Messrs. Bosanquets' and J. Fatio's sugar-plantation in their partners' absence. Finding at length the unprofitable way in which the West Indian planters conducted their concerns, he returned to the East Indies in 1776, and established sugar-works at Bencoolen on his own account. Being in London in the year 1789, when a committee of privy council was sitting to examine into the question of the slave trade, he delivered a paper to the board on the mode of cultivating a sugar plantation in the East Indies; and this paper being thought of great importance, he was summoned afterwards in 1791 by a committee of the House of Commons to be examined personally upon it.

It is very remarkable that the very first sentence in this paper announced the fact at once, that "sugar, better and *cheaper* than that in the West Indian islands, was produced *by free men.*"

Mr. Botham then explained the simple process of making sugar in the East. "A proprietor, generally a Dutchman, used to let his estate, say 300 acres or more, with proper buildings upon it, to a Chinese, who lived upon it and superintended it, and who re-let it to free men in parcels of 50 or 60 acres on condition that they should plant it in canes for so much for every pecul, 133 lbs., of sugar produced. This superintendant hired people from the adjacent villages to take off his crop. One lot of task-men with their carts and buffaloes cut the canes, carried them to the mill, and ground them. A second set boiled them, and a third clayed and basketed them for market at so much per pecul. Thus the renter knew with certainty what every pecul would cost him, and he incurred no unnecessary expense; for, when the crop was over, the task-men returned home. By dividing the labour in this manner, it was better and cheaper done."

Mr. Botham detailed next the improved method of making sugar in Batavia, which we have not room to insert here. We may just state, however, that the persons concerned in it never made spirits on the sugar estates. The molasses and skimmings were sent for, sale to Batavia, where one distillery might buy the produce of a hundred estates. Here, again, was a vast saving, says Mr. Botham, "there was not, as in the West Indies, a *distillery* for *each estate.*"

He then proceeded to make a comparison between the agricultural system of the two countries. "The cane was cultivated *to the utmost perfection* in Batavia, whereas the culture of it in the West Indies was but *in its infancy. The hoe was scarcely used* in the East, whereas it was almost *the sole implement* in the West. The *plough was used instead of it in the East,* as far as it could be done. Young canes there were kept also often ploughed as a weeding, and the hoe was kept to weed round the plant when very young; but of this there was little need, if the land had been sufficiently ploughed. When the cane was ready to be earthed up, it was done by a *sort of shovel* made for the purpose. *Two persons* with this instrument would earth up more canes in a day than *ten Negroes* with hoes. The cane-roots were also *ploughed up* in the East, whereas they were *dug up with the severest exertion* in the West. Many alterations," says Mr. Botham, "are to be made, and expenses and human labour lessened in the West. *Having experienced the difference of labourers for profit and labourers from force*, I can assert, that *the savings by the former are very considerable.*"

He then pointed out other defects in the West Indian management, and their remedies. "I am of opinion," says he, "that the West Indian planter should for his own interest give more labour to beast and less to man. A larger portion of his estate ought to be in pasture. When practicable, canes should be carried to the mill, and cane tops and grass to the stock, in waggons. The custom of making a hard-worked Negro get a bundle of grass twice a day should be abolished, and in short a *total change take place in the miserable management in our West Indian Islands*. By these means following as near as possible the East Indian mode, and consolidating the distilleries, I do suppose our sugar-islands might be better worked than they now are by *two-thirds* or indeed *one-half* of the present force. Let it be considered how much labour is lost by the persons *overseeing the forced labourer*, which is saved when he works *for his own profit*. I have stated with the strictest veracity a plain matter of fact, that sugar estates can *be worked cheaper by free men than by slaves*[16]."

I shall now show, that the old maxim, which has been mentioned, is true, when applied to the case of our West Indian islands, by establishing a fact of a very different kind, viz. that the slaves in the West Indies do much more work in a given time when *they work for themselves*, than when *they work for their masters*. But how, it will be said, do you prove, by establishing this fact, that it would be cheaper for our planters to employ free men than slaves? I answer thus: I maintain that, *while the slaves are working for themselves*, they are to be considered, indeed that they are, *bonâ fide, free labourers*. In the first place, they never have a driver with them on any of these occasions; and, in the second place, *having all their earnings to themselves*, they have that stimulus within them to excite industry, which is only known *to free men*. What is it, I ask, which gives birth to industry in any part of the world, seeing that labour is not agreeable to man, but the stimulus arising from the hope of gain? What makes an English labourer do more work in the day than a slave, but the stimulus arising from the knowledge, that what he earns is *for himself and not for another*? What, again, makes an English labourer do much more work *by the piece* than by *the day*, but the stimulus arising from the knowledge that he may gain more by the former than by the latter mode of work? Just so is the West Indian slave situated, when *he is working for himself*, that is, when he knows *that what he earns is for his own use*. He has then all the stimulus of a free man, and he is, therefore, *during such work* (though unhappily no longer) really, and in effect, and to all intents and purposes, as much *a free labourer* as any person in any part of the globe. But if he be a free man, while he is working for himself, and if in that capacity he does twice or thrice more work than when he works for his master, it follows, that it would be cheaper for his master to employ him as a free labourer, or that the labour of free men in the West Indies would be cheaper than the labour of slaves.

That West Indian slaves, when they work for themselves, do much more in a given time than when they work for their masters, is a fact so notorious in the West Indies, that no one who has been there would deny it. Look at Long's History of Jamaica, The Privy Council Report, Gaisford's Essay on the good Effects of the Abolition of the Slave Trade, and other books. Let us hear also what Dr. Dickson, the editor of Mr. Steele, and who resided so many years in Barbadoes, says on this subject, for what he says is so admirably expressed that I cannot help quoting it. "The planters," says he, "do not take the right way to make human beings put forth their strength. They apply main force where they should apply moral motives, and punishments alone where rewards should be judiciously intermixed. They first beslave their poor people with their cursed whip, and then stand and wonder at the tremour of their nerves, and the laxity of their muscles. And yet, strange to tell, *those very men affirm, and affirm truly*, that a slave will do more work for himself *in an afternoon* than he can be made to do for his owner *in a whole day or more!*" And did not the whole Assembly of Grenada, as we collect from the famous speech of Mr. Pitt on the Slave Trade in 1791, affirm the same thing? "He (Mr. Pitt) would show," he said, "the futility of the argument of his honourable friend. He (his honourable friend) had himself admitted, that it was in the power of the colonies to correct the various abuses by which the Negro population was restrained. But they could not do this without *improving the condition of their slaves*, without making them *approximate towards the rank of citizens*, without giving them *some little interest in their labour*, which would occasion them to work *with the energy of men*. But now the Assembly of Grenada had themselves stated, that, *though the Negroes were allowed the afternoon of only one day in every week, they would do as much work in that afternoon when employed for their own benefit, as in the whole day when employed in their masters' service*. Now after this confession the House might burn all his calculations relative to the Negro population; for if this population had not quite reached the desirable state which he had pointed out, this confession had proved that further supplies were not wanted. A Negro, *if he worked for himself, could do double work*. By an improvement then in the mode of labour, the work in the islands could be doubled. But if so, what would become of the argument of his honourable friend? for then only half the number of the present labourers were necessary."

But the fact, that the slaves in the West Indies do much more work for themselves in a given time than when they work for their masters, may be established almost arithmetically, if we will take the trouble of calculating from authentic documents which present themselves on the subject. It is surprising, when we look into the evidence examined by the House of

Commons on the subject of the Slave Trade, to find how little a West Indian slave really does, when he works for his master; and this is confessed equally by the witnesses on both sides of the question. One of them (Mr. Francklyn) says, that a labouring man could not get his bread in Europe if he worked no harder than a Negro. Another (Mr. Tobin), that no Negro works like a day-labourer in England. Another (Sir John Dalling), that the general work of Negroes is not to be called labour. A fourth (Dr. Jackson), that an English labourer does three times as much work as a Negro in the West Indies. Now how are these expressions to be reconciled with the common notions in England of Negro labour? for "to work like a Negro" is a common phrase, which is understood to convey the meaning, that the labour of the Negroes is the most severe and intolerable that is known. One of the witnesses, however, just mentioned explains the matter. "The hardship," says he, "of Negro field-labour is more in the *mode* than in the *quantity* done. The slave, seeing no end of his labour, stands over the work, and only throws the hoe to avoid the lash. He appears to work without actually working." The truth is, that a Negro, having no interest in his work while working for his master, will work only while the whip is upon him. I can no where make out the clear net annual earnings of a field Negro on a sugar plantation to come up to 8*l.* sterling. Now what does he earn in the course of a year when he is working for himself? I dare not repeat what some of the witnesses for the planters stated to the House of Commons, when representing the enviable condition of the slaves in the West Indies; for this would be to make him earn more for himself *in one day* than for his master *in a week.* Let us take then the lowest sum mentioned in the Book of Evidence. This is stated to be 14*d.* sterling per week; and 14*d.* sterling per week would make 3*l.* sterling per year. But how many days in the week does he work when he makes such annual earnings? The most time, which any of the witnesses gives to a field slave for his own private concerns, is every Sunday, and also every Saturday afternoon in the week, besides three holidays in the year. But this is far from being the general account. Many of them say that he has only Sunday to himself; and others, that even Sunday is occasionally trespassed upon by his master. It appears, also, that even where the afternoon is given him, it is only out of crop-time. Now let us take into the account the time lost by slaves in going backwards and forwards to their provision-grounds; for though some of these are described as being only a stone's throw from their huts, others are described as being one, and two, and three, and even four miles off; and let us take into the account also, that Sunday is, by the confession of all, the Negro market day, on which alone they can dispose of their own produce, and that the market itself may be from one to ten or fifteen miles from their homes, and that they who go there cannot be working in their gardens at the same time, and we shall find that there cannot be on an average more than a clear three quarters of a day in the week, which they can call their own, and in which they can work for themselves. But call it a whole day, if you please, and you will find that the slave does for himself in this one day more than a third of what he does for his master in six, or that he works *more than three times harder* when *he works for himself* than when *he works for his master.*

I have now shown, first by the evidence of Mr. Botham, and secondly by the fact of Negroes earning more in a given time when they work in their own gardens, than when they work in their master's service, that the old maxim "of *its being cheaper to employ free men than slaves,*" is true, when applied to the *operations and demands of West Indian agriculture.* But if it be cheaper to employ free men than slaves in the West Indies, then they, who should emancipate their Negroes there, would *promote their interest by so doing.* "But hold!" says an objector, "we allow that their successors would be benefited, but not the *emancipators themselves.* These would have a great sacrifice to make. Their slaves are worth so much money at this moment; but they would lose all this value, if they were to set them free." I reply, and indeed I have all along affirmed, that it is not proposed to emancipate the slaves *at once,* but to prepare them for emancipation *in a course of years.* Mr. Steele did not make his slaves *entirely free.* They were *copyhold-bond slaves.* They were still *his freehold property*: and they would, if he had lived, have continued so for many years. They therefore, who should emancipate, would lose nothing of the value of their slaves, so long as they brought them only to the door of liberty, but did not allow them to pass through it. But suppose they were to allow them to pass through it and thus admit them to freedom, they would lose nothing by so doing; for they would not admit them to freedom till *after a certain period of years, during which* I contend that the *value of every individual slave* would have been *reimbursed* to them from *the increased income of their estates.* Mr. Steele, as we have seen, *more than tripled* the value of his income during his experiment: I believe that he more than quadrupled it; for he says, that he more than tripled it *besides increasing his stock,* and *laying out large sums annually in adding necessary works,* and *in repairs of the damage by the great hurricane.* Suppose then a West India estate to yield at this moment a nett income of 500*l.* per annum, this income would be increased, according to Mr. Steele's experience, to somewhere about 1700*l.* per annum. Would not, then, the surplus beyond the original 500*l.*, viz. 1200*l.* per annum, be sufficient to reimburse the proprietor in a few years for the value of every slave which he had when he began his plan of emancipation? But he would be reimbursed again, that is, (twice over on the whole for every individual slave,) from a new source, viz. *the improved value of his land.* It is a fact well known in the United States, that a certain quantity of land, or farm, in full cultivation by free men, will fetch twice more money than the same quantity of land, similarly circumstanced, in full cultivation by slaves. Let us suppose now that the slaves at present on any West Indian plantation are worth about as much as the land with the buildings upon it, to which they are attached, and that the land with the buildings upon it would rise to double its former value when cultivated by free men, it follows that the land and buildings alone would be worth as much then, that is, when worked by free labourers, as the land, buildings, and slaves together are worth at the present time.

I have now, I think, pretty well canvassed the subject, and I shall therefore hasten to a conclusion. And first, I ask the West Indians, whether they think that they will be allowed to carry on their present cruel system, the arbitrary use of the whip and the chain, and the brutal debasement of their fellow-creatures, *for ever.* I say, No; I entertain better hopes of the humanity and justice of the British people. I am sure that they will interfere, and that when they *once take up the cause,* they *will never abandon it till they have obtained their object.* And what is it, after all, that I have been proposing in the course of the preceding pages? two things only, viz. that the laws relating to the slaves may be revised by the British parliament, so that they, may be made (as it was always intended) *to accord with, and not to be repugnant to,* the principles of the British constitution, and that, when such a revision shall have taken place, the slaves may be put into *a state of preparation for emancipation*; and for such an emancipation only as may be compatible with the joint interests of the master and the slave. Is there any thing unreasonable in this proposition? Is it unreasonable to desire that those laws should be repealed, which are contrary to the laws of God, or that the Africans and their descendants, who have the shape, image, intellect, feelings, and affections of men, should be treated as human beings?

The measure then, which I have been proposing, is *not unreasonable.* I trust it *would not be injurious* to the interests of the West Indians themselves. These are at present, it is said, in great distress; and so they have been for years; and so they will still be (and moreover they will be getting worse and worse) *so long as they continue slavery.* How can such a wicked, such an ill-framed system succeed? Has not the Almighty in his moral government of the world stamped a character upon human actions, and given such a turn to their operations, that the balance should be ultimately in favour of virtue? Has he not taken from those, who act wickedly, the power of discerning the right path? or has he not so confounded their faculties, that they are for ever frustrating their own schemes? It is only to know the practice of our planters to be assured, that it will bring on difficulty after difficulty, and loss after loss, till it will end in ruin. If a man were to sit down and to try to invent a ruinous system of agriculture, could he devise one more to his mind than that which they have been in the habit of using? Let us look at some of the more striking parts of this system. The first that stares us in the face, is the unnatural and destructive practice of *forced labour.* Here we see men working without any rational stimulus to elicit their exertions, and therefore they must be followed by drivers with whips in their hands. Well might it be said by Mr. Botham to the Committees of Privy-council and House of Commons, "Let it be considered, how much labour is lost by the persons overseeing the forced labourer, which is saved when he works for his own profit;" and, notwithstanding all the vigilance and whipping of these drivers, I have proved that the slaves do more for themselves in an afternoon, than in a whole day when they work for their masters. It was doubtless the conviction that *forced labour was unprofitable*, as well as that there would be less of human suffering, which made Mr. Steele take away the whips from his drivers, as *the very first step necessary* in his improved system, or as the *sine quâ non* without which such a system could not properly be begun; and did not this very measure *alter the face of his affairs in point of profit in three years after it had been put into operation*? And here it must be observed, that, if ever emancipation should be begun by our planters, this must be (however they may dislike to part with arbitrary power) as much a first step with them as it was with Mr. Steele. *Forced labour* stands at the head of the catalogue of those nuisances belonging to slavery, which oppose the planter's gain. It must be removed before any thing else can be done. See what mischiefs it leads to, independently of its want of profit. It is impossible that forced labour can be kept up from day to day without injury to the constitution of the slaves; and if their health is injured, the property of their masters must be injured also. Forced labour, again, sends many of them to the sick-houses. Here is, at any rate, a loss of their working time. But it drives them also occasionally to run away, and sometimes to destroy themselves. Here again is a loss of their working time and of property into the bargain. *Forced labour*, then, is one of those striking parts in the West Indian husbandry, in which we see a *constant source of loss* to those who adopt it; and may we not speak, and yet with truth, as unfavourably of some of the other striking parts in the same system? What shall we say, first, to that injurious disproportion of the articles of croppage with the wants of the estates, which makes little or no provision of food for the labourers (*the very first to be cared for*), but leaves these to be fed by articles to be bought three thousand miles off in another country, let the markets there be ever so high, or the prices ever so unfavourable, at the time? What shall we say, again, to that obstinate and ruinous attachment to old customs, in consequence of which even acknowledged improvements are almost forbidden to be received? How generally has the introduction of the plough been opposed in the West Indies, though both the historians of Jamaica have recommended the use of it, and though it has been proved that *one plough* with *two sets of horses* to relieve each other, would turn up as much land *in a day, as one hundred Negroes* could with their hoes! Is not the hoe also continued in earthing up the canes there, when Mr. Botham proved, more than thirty years ago, that *two* men would do more with the East Indian shovel at that sort of work in a day, than *ten* Negroes with the former instrument? So much for *unprofitable instruments* of husbandry; a few words now on *unprofitable modes of employment.* It seems, first, little less than infatuation, to make Negroes carry baskets of dung upon their heads, basket after basket, to the field. I do not mention this so much as an intolerable hardship upon those who have to perform it, as an improvident waste of strength and time. Why are not horses, or mules, or oxen, and carts or other vehicles of convenience, used oftener on such occasions? I may notice also that cruel and most disadvantageous mode of employment of making Negroes collect grass for the cattle, by picking it by the hand blade by blade. Are no artificial grasses to be found in our islands, and is the existence of the scythe unknown there? But it is of no use to dwell longer upon this subject. The whole system is a ruinous one from the beginning to the end. And from whence does such a system arise? It has its origin in *slavery* alone. It is practised no where but in the land of ignorance and slavery. Slavery indeed, or rather the despotism which supports slavery, has no compassion, and it is one of its characteristics *never to think of sparing the sinews of the wretched creature called a slave.* Hence it is slow to adopt helps, with which a beneficent Providence has furnished us, by giving to man an inventive faculty for easing his burthens, or by submitting the beasts of the field to his dominion and his use, and it flies to expedients which are contrary to nature and reason. How then can such a system ever answer? Were an English farmer to have recourse to such a system, he would not be able to pay his rent for a single year. If the planters then are in distress, it is their own fault. They may, however, thank the abolitionists that they are not worse off than they are at present. The abolition of the slave trade, by cutting off the purchase of new slaves, has cut off one cause of their ruin[17]; and it is only the abolition *of slavery which can yet save them.* Had the planters, when the slave trade was abolished, taken immediate measures to meet the change; had they then revised their laws and substituted better; had they then put their slaves into a state of preparation for emancipation, in what a different, that is, desirable situation would they have been at this moment! In fact, *nothing can save them, but the abolition of slavery on a wise and prudent plan.* They can no more expect, without it, to meet the present low prices of colonial produce, than the British farmer can meet the present low prices of grain, unless he can have an abatement of rent, tithe, and taxation, and unless his present poor rates can be diminished also. Take away, however, from the planters the use and practice of slavery, and the hour of *their regeneration* would be begun. Can we doubt, that Providence would then bless their endeavours, and that *salvation* from their difficulties would be their portion in the end?

It has appeared, I hope, by this time, that what I have been proposing is not unreasonable, and that, so far from being injurious to the interests of the planters, it would be highly advantageous to them. I shall now show, that I do not ask for the introduction of a more humane system into our Colonies *at a time when it would be improper to grant it;* or that no fair objection can be raised against the *present moment,* as *the fit era* from whence the measures in contemplation should commence. There was, indeed, a time when the planters might have offered something like an excuse for the severity of their conduct towards their slaves, on the plea that the greater part of them then in the colonies were *African-born* or *strangers*, and that cargoes were constantly pouring in, one after the other, consisting of the same sort of beings; or of *stubborn ferocious people, never accustomed to work, whose spirits it was necessary to break*, and *whose necks to force down to the yoke*; and that this could only be effected by the whip, the chain, the iron collar, and other instruments of the kind. But *now* no such plea can be offered. It is now sixteen years since the slave trade was abolished by England, and it is therefore to be presumed, that no new slaves have been imported into the British colonies within that period. The slaves, therefore, who are there at this day, must consist either of Africans, whose spirits must have been long ago broken, or of Creoles born in the cradle and brought up in the trammels of slavery. What argument then can be produced for the continuation of a barbarous discipline there? And we are very glad to find that two gentlemen, both of whom we have had occasion to quote before, bear us out in this remark. Mr. Steele, speaking of some of the old cruel laws of Barbadoes, applies them to the case before us in these words:—"As, according to Ligon's account, there were not above two-thirds of the island in plantations in the year 1650, we must suppose that in the year 1688 the great number of *African-born* slaves brought into the plantations in chains, and compelled to labour by the terrors of corporal punishment, might have made it appear necessary to enact a temporary law so harsh as the statute No. 82; but when the *great majority* of the Negroes were become *vernacular, born in the island, naturalized by language,* and *familiarised by custom,* did not *policy* as well as humanity require: them *to be put under milder conditions*, such as were granted to the slaves of our Saxon ancestors?" Colonel Malenfant speaks the same sentiments. In defending his plan, which he offered to the French Government for St. Domingo in 1814, against the vulgar prejudice, that "where you employ Negroes you must of necessity use slavery," he delivers himself thus:—"[18]If all the Negroes on a plantation had not been more than six months out of Africa, or if they had the same ideas concerning an independent manner of life as the Indians or the savages of Guiana, I should consider my plan to be impracticable. I should then say that coercion would be necessary: but ninety-nine out of every hundred Negroes in St. Domingo are aware that they cannot obtain necessaries without work. They know that it is their duty to work, and they are even desirous of working; but the remembrance of their cruel sufferings in the time of slavery renders them suspicious." We may conclude, then, that if a cruel discipline was *not necessary* in the years 1790 and 1794, to which these gentlemen allude, when there must have been *some thousands of newly imported Africans* both in St. Domingo and in the English colonies, it cannot be necessary *now*, when there have been no importations into the latter for *fifteen years*. There can be no excuse, then, for the English planters for not altering their system, and this *immediately*. It is, on the other hand, a great reproach to them, considering the quality and character of their slaves, *that they should not of themselves have come forward on the subject before this time.*

Seeing then that nothing has been done where it ought, it is the duty of the abolitionists to *resume their labours.* If through the medium of the abolition of the slave trade they have not accomplished, as they expected, the whole of their object, they have no alternative but to resort to *other measures*, or to attempt by constitutional means, under that Legislature which has already sanctioned their efforts, the mitigation of the cruel treatment of the Negroes, with the ultimate view of extinguishing, in due time and in a suitable manner, the slavery itself. Nor ought any time to be lost in making such an attempt; for it is a melancholy fact, that there is scarcely any increase of the slave population in our islands at the present moment. What other proof need we require *of the severity of the slavery there, and of the necessity of its mitigation?* Severe punishments, want of sufficient food, labour extracted by the whip, and a system of prostitution, conspire, *almost as much as ever*, to make inroads upon the constitutions of the slaves, and to prevent their increase. And let it be remembered here, that any former defect of this kind was supplied by importations; but that importations are *now unlawful.* Unless, therefore, the abolitionists interfere, and that soon, our West Indian planters may come to Parliament and say, "We have now tried your experiment. It has not answered. You must therefore give us leave to go again to the coast of Africa for slaves." There is also another consideration worthy of the attention of the abolitionists, viz. that *a public attempt* made in England to procure the abolition of *slavery* would very much promote their original object, the cause of the abolition of the slave trade; for foreign courts have greatly doubted our sincerity as to the latter measure, and have therefore been very backward in giving us their assistance in it. If England, say they, abolished the slave trade *from moral motives*, how happens it *that she continues slavery?* But if this *public attempt* were to succeed, then the abolitionists would see their wishes in a direct train for completion: for if slavery were to fall in the British islands, this event would occasion death in a given time, and without striking any further blow, to the execrable trade in every part of the world; because those foreigners, who should continue slavery, no longer able to compete in the markets with those who should employ free men, must abandon the slave trade altogether.

But here perhaps the planters will say, "What right have the people of England to interfere with our property, which would be the case if they were to attempt to abolish slavery?" The people of England might reply, that they have as good a right as you, the planters, have to interfere with that most precious of all property, *the liberty of your slaves*, seeing that *you hold them by no right that is not opposed to nature, reason, justice, and religion.* The people of England have no desire to interfere with your *property*, but with your *oppression.* It is probable that your property would be improved by the change. But, to examine this right more minutely, I contend, first, that they have always a right to interfere in behalf of humanity and justice wherever their appeals can be heard. I contend, secondly, that they have a more immediate right to interfere in the present case, because the oppressed persons in question, living in the British dominions and under the British Government, are *their fellow subjects.* I contend again, that they have this right upon the ground that they are giving you, the West Indians, *a monopoly* for their sugar, by buying it from you exclusively *at a much dearer rate* than *they can get it from other quarters.* Surely they have a right to say to you, as customers for your produce, Change your system and we will continue to deal with you; but if you will not change it, we will buy our sugar elsewhere, or we will not buy sugar at all. The East Indian market is open to us, and we prefer sugar that is not stained with blood. Nay, we will petition Parliament to take off the surplus duty with which East Indian sugar is loaded on your account. What superior claims have you either upon Parliament or upon us, that you should have the preference? As to the East Indians, they are as much the subjects of the British empire as yourselves. As to the East India Company, they support all their establishments, both civil and military, at their own expense. They come to our Treasury for nothing; while you, with naval stations, and an extraordinary military force kept up for no other purpose than to keep in awe an injured population, and with heavy bounties on the exportation of your sugar, put us to such an expense as makes us doubt whether your trade is worth having on its present terms. They, the East India Company, again, have been a blessing to the Natives with whom they have been concerned. They distribute an equal system of law and justice to all without respect of persons. They dispell the clouds of ignorance, superstition, and idolatry, and carry with them civilization and liberty wherever they go. You, on the other hand, have no code of justice but for yourselves. You *deny it* to those who *cannot help themselves.* You *hinder liberty* by your cruel restrictions on manumission; and dreading the inlet of light, *you study to perpetuate ignorance and barbarism.* Which then of the two competitors has the claim to preference by an English Parliament and an English people? It may probably soon become a question with the latter, whether they will consent to pay a million annually more for West India sugar than for other of like quality, or, which is the same thing, whether they will allow themselves to be *taxed annually to the amount of a million sterling to support West Indian slavery.*

I shall now conclude by saying, that I leave it; and that I recommend it, to others to add to the light which I have endeavoured to furnish on this subject, by collecting new facts relative to Emancipation and the result of it in other parts of the world, as well as relative to the superiority of free over servile labour, in order that the West Indians may be convinced, if possible, that they would be benefited by the change of system which I propose. They must already know, both by past and present experience, that the ways of unrighteousness are not profitable. Let them not doubt, when the Almighty has decreed the balance in favour of virtuous actions, that their efforts under the new system will work together for their good, so that their temporal redemption may be at hand.

THE END.

FOOTNOTES:

[1] See Dickson's Mitigation of Slavery, p. 18.

[2] See Dickson's Mitigation of Slavery, p. 339.

[3] Mitigation of Slavery, p. 50.

[4] See Dickson's Mitigation of Slavery, p. 102.

[5] A part of the black regiments were bought in Africa as recruits, and were not transported in slave-ships, and, never under West India masters: but it was only a small part compared with the whole number in the three cases.

[6] Mémoire historique et politique des Colonies, et particulièrement de celle de St. Domingue, &c. Paris, August 1814. 8vo. p. 58.

[7] Pp. 125, 126.

[8] There were occasionally marauding parties from the mountains, who pillaged in the plains; but these were the old insurgent, and not the emancipated Negroes.

[9] P. 78.

[10] Mémoires, p. 311.

[11] Ibid. p. 324.

[12] The French were not the authors of tearing to pieces the Negroes alive by bloodhounds, or of suffocating them by hundreds at a time in the holds of ships, or of drowning them (whole cargoes) by scuttling and sinking the vessels;—but the *planters*.

[13] All the slave-population was to be emancipated in 18 years; and this consisted at the time of passing the decree of from 250,000 to 300,000 souls.

[14] See Dr. Dickson's Mitigation of Slavery, London 1814, from whence every thing relating to this subject is taken. Dr. Dickson had been for many years secretary to Governor Hay, in Barbadoes, where he had an opportunity of studying the Slave agriculture as a system. Being in London afterwards when the Slave Trade controversy was going on in Parliament, he distinguished himself by silencing the different writers who defended the West Indian slavery. There it was that Mr. Steele addressed himself to him by letter, and sent him those invaluable papers, which the Doctor afterwards published under the modest title of "Mitigation of Slavery by Steele and Dickson." No one was better qualified than Dr. Dickson to become the Editor of Mr. Steele.

[15] It is much to be feared that this beautiful order of things was broken up after Mr. Steele's death by his successors, either through their own prejudices, or their unwillingness or inability to stand against the scoffs and prejudices of others. It may be happy, however, for thousands now in slavery, that Mr. Steele lived to accomplish his plan. The constituent parts and result of it being known, a fine example is shown to those who may be desirous of trying emancipation.

[16] Mr. Botham's account is confirmed incontrovertibly by the fact, that sugar made in the East Indies can be brought to England (though it has three times the distance to come, and of course three times the freight to pay), and yet be afforded to the consumer at as cheap a rate as any that can be brought thither from the West.

[17] Dickson's Mitigation of Slavery, p. 213, where it is proved that bought slaves never refund their purchase-money to their owners.

[18] P. 125.